P9-CQW-693

The Tragedy of

KING LEAR

with Related Readings

THE GLOBAL SHAKESPEARE SERIES

The Tragedy of
KING LEAR

with Related Readings

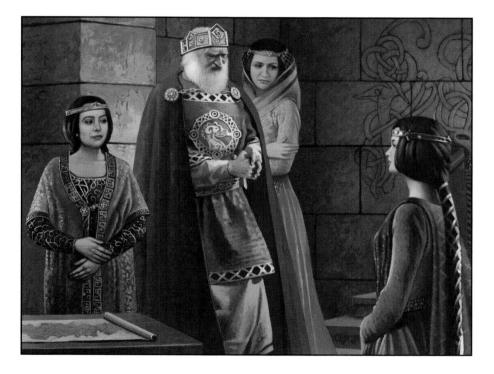

SERIES EDITORS

Dom Saliani   **Chris Ferguson**   **Dr. Tim Scott**

I(T)P *International Thomson Publishing*

Albany • Bonn • Boston • Cincinnati • Detroit • London • Madrid • Melbourne • Mexico City •
New York • Pacific Grove • Paris • San Francisco • Singapore • Tokyo • Toronto • Washington

I(T)P™
International Thomson Publishing, 1998

All rights in this book are reserved.
The text of this publication, or any part thereof, may not be reproduced or transmitted in any form or by any means, electronic or mechanical, including photocopying, storage in an information retrieval system, or otherwise, without the prior written permission of the publisher.

The trademark ITP is used under licence.

Published simultaneously by International Thomson Limited:

ITP Nelson (Canada)   **South-Western Educational Publishing (U.S.A.)**
Nelson ITP (Australia)   **Thomas Nelson United Kingdom**

www.thomson.com

ISBN 0-17-606621-7

Cataloguing in Publication Data

Shakespeare, William, 1564-1616
    [King Lear]
  King Lear with related readings

(The global Shakespeare series)
ISBN 0-17-606621-7

1. Shakespeare, William, 1564-1616. King Lear.
I. Title.   II. Title: King Lear.   III. Series

PR2819.A1 1997   822.3'3   C97-931250-7

Acquisitions Editor:	TARA STEELE
Project Managers:	JAN HARKNESS (CANADA)
	JACKIE TIDEY (AUSTRALIA)
	LAURIE WENDELL (U.S.A.)
Series Designer:	LIZ HARASYMCZUK
Developmental Editor:	DAVID FRIEND
Production Editor:	SANDRA MANLEY
Sr. Composition Analyst:	DARYN DEWALT
Production Coordinator:	THERESA THOMAS
Permissions Editor:	JILL YOUNG
Cover Illustrator:	YUAN LEE
Research:	LISA BRANT
Film:	IMAGING EXCELLENCE

Printed and bound in Canada
1 2 3 4 5 ML 01 00 99 98 97

Contents

Features of the *Global Shakespeare Series*

— ❧ —

Introduction to the Play: Information on the date, sources, themes, and appeal of the play, notes on Shakespeare's use of verse and prose, and common stage directions all help to set a context for the play.

The Text: The *Global Shakespeare Series* is faithful to Shakespeare's full original texts. Spelling and punctuation have been modernized to make the plays accessible to today's readers. For the last 200 years, many editors have chosen to arrange and rearrange Shakespeare's words to create a consistent iambic pentameter in the text. For example, a dialogue involving short speeches would look like this:

LEAR: Come, let's in all.
KENT: This way, my lord.
LEAR: With him!

Together the three lines make up 10 syllables. In some cases, editors have even taken words from one line and combined them with words from another line to create the iambic pentameter pattern. Shakespeare did not do this in his original text. The *Global Shakespeare Series* has not adopted this convention. What you see is what Shakespeare wrote.

Dramatis Personae: The list of characters is organized by families or by loyalty affiliations.

Scene Summaries: Brief synopses help you to follow and anticipate developments in the plot.

Artwork and Graphics: Original artwork has been created and designed for this series by internationally acclaimed artists.

Marginal Notes: Generous notes define difficult or archaic vocabulary. In some cases, entire sentences of Shakespeare are paraphrased into modern idiom — these are identified with quotation marks.

Notes of Interest: Longer notes provide background information on Shakespeare's times or interesting interpretations of various speeches or characters.

Quotable Notables: Brief comments on various aspects of the play by authors, celebrities, and highly regarded literary critics and professors are included. The views do not necessarily reflect the views of the editors; they are merely springboards for discussion, debate, and reflection.

Related Reading References: These references indicate that there is a piece of literature in the latter part of the book that relates well to a specific scene or speech.

Considerations: Each Act is followed by a series of scene-specific "considerations." Some involve analysis and interpretation; others will offer opportunities to be creative and imaginative.

Related Readings: The second half of the text contains poems, short stories, short drama, and non-fiction pieces that are directly related to the play. These can be read for enjoyment or for enrichment. They emphasize the continuing relevance of Shakespeare in today's society.

Ten Challenging Questions: These questions are ideal for developing into research or independent study projects.

Introduction to *King Lear*

— ❧ —

Appeal of *King Lear*

Poet Percy Bysshe Shelley considered *King Lear* to be "the most perfect specimen of the dramatic art existing in the world." In praising the play, Charles Lamb stated that "the Lear of Shakespeare cannot be acted." Scholar A.C. Bradley echoed this sentiment by describing the play as being "too huge for the stage."

King Lear occupies a unique position in the Shakespearean canon. It is considered to be one of his greatest works as well as one of the most troubling. Many readers and audiences are horrified by the cruelty and savagery in the plot and many are troubled by its pessimism and hopelessness. Others, however, are moved by the humanity and kindness expressed by various characters in the play. To these readers, the play is hopeful in that it marks the beginnings of a civilized culture in Britain.

Lear offers a range of human emotions and qualities. It can be seen as a study of madness; but it also traces Lear's growth as he becomes a more caring individual. One scholar has even suggested that the title of the play should be *The Redemption of King Lear*. Lear's world is not all violence and savagery. It also contains the love, forgiveness, and kindness shown by Cordelia, Edgar, and several of the servants.

The Double Plot of *King Lear*

Paralleling the main story line of Lear and his daughters is a fully developed subplot of the Earl of Gloucester and his sons. The two plots are so intricately intertwined that it would be difficult to imagine the play without this story. As you read *King Lear*, note the great care Shakespeare has taken to draw parallels between the two stories.

King Lear — Legend or History?

According to legend (and several unsubstantiated historical references), King Lear ruled Britain at about the same time as Judea was ruled by kings — 800 B.C.E. Lear was supposedly a direct descendant of King Brut, the legendary founder of the kingdom of Britain.

During Shakespeare's time, however, people were more interested in the story of Edgar than that of Lear. The story of Lear would have reminded audiences of the grave dangers of a divided kingdom. Most of Shakespeare's history plays warned of the dangers of treason and the horrors of civil war. It was the story of Edgar that captured the people's imagination in that the reign of the legendary King Edgar marked an important beginning in English history. According to tradition, it was Edgar who brought social order and political stability to the island, civilizing the people and bringing them out of a barbaric, violent prehistory.

Some scholars even suggest that *King Lear* is the first in the cycle of English history plays in that it dramatizes the beginnings of British civilization.

Sources of the Play

Scholars have counted more than forty works that Shakespeare may have consulted in writing his *King Lear*. The following represent his major sources:

Geoffrey of Monmouth – *Historia Regum Britanniae* (1137)
Holinshed's *Chronicles* (1577)
Edmund Spenser – *The Faerie Queene* (1590)
John Higgins – *A Mirror for Magistrates* (1574)
Sir Philip Sidney – *Arcadia* (1590)

Records show that in 1594, a *king leare* was performed at the Rose Theatre. There is no agreement on who authored this early version of the play. In 1605, the anonymously written *King Leir* appeared in print. Many scholars believe that Shakespeare used this later play as his source. Some, however, contend that the 1594 play may have been an early Shakespearean version of the play upon which the later *King Leir* was based. It was not uncommon for dramatists to revise their work frequently over the years, and this may have been the case with Shakespeare's *King Lear*.

What all the sources of the play have in common, without exception, is that they all end happily. Why Shakespeare so radically changed the ending of the story will forever remain a mystery, but in so doing he created one of the greatest tragedies of all time.

Rewriting *Lear*

It is a matter of historical record that Shakespeare's version of the Lear story was not a popular one. In fact, it was not performed at all between 1681 and 1838. In its place, a happy ending *Lear* entertained audiences who considered Shakespeare's version too dark, too savage, and too tragic.

Nahum Tate, the author of this popular rewrite, considered Shakespeare's *King Lear* to be a "Heap of Jewels, unstrung and unpolished." In his version, Cordelia survives, marries Edgar, and together with Edgar rules over England. (See page 175 of the Related Readings for Tate's happy ending.)

Scholars and readers have scoffed at the notion of changing the ending of Shakespeare's *King Lear* to give it a happier resolution. Nonetheless, the fact remains that Shakespeare's sources end happily with Lear regaining his throne, living for several years, and then being succeeded by Cordelia.

Tate may have created a popular entertainment, but Shakespeare created an enduring masterpiece that continues to excite the imaginations of readers and audiences.

Date and Text of the Play

Scholars are divided about when the play was actually written. Some place the composition date as early as 1594 and others as late as 1603. *King Lear* appeared in *quarto* form in 1608. A quarto is a book produced by folding large sheets into four before binding the sheets together. The title page of the 1608 Quarto edition suggests that *King Lear* was performed for King James on December 26, 1606.

In 1623, thirty-six of Shakespeare's plays were collected and printed in a volume now referred to as the First Folio. This volume included a version of *King Lear* that was dramatically different from the 1608 Quarto version.

It has been debated ever since which version is more authoritative. The problem is that the quarto contains approximately 300 lines that are not in the Folio edition, and the Folio contains approximately 100 lines not in the Quarto. There are also many words throughout the two versions that are different.

The edition for this text is *conflated*. This means that this text contains all the lines found in the two versions. When there is a variation in the choice of words, this edition follows the Folio version more often than not. Spelling and punctuation have been modernized to make the reading more accessible to today's readers.

Shakespeare's Verse and Prose

Many students find Shakespeare difficult to read and understand. They often ask whether or not the Elizabethans spoke the way Shakespeare's characters do. The answer is, of course, no. Shakespeare wrote using a poetic form known as *blank verse*. This produces an elevated style of speech that would have been very different from everyday speech during the Elizabethan period.

Furthermore, the blank verse contains a rhythm pattern known as *iambic pentameter*. This means that most lines contain five feet (a pentameter) and each foot contains an unstressed and a stressed syllable (an iamb). In other words, as Shakespeare wrote, playing in the back of his mind was a rhythm pattern that would sound like this:

da DA da DA da DA da DA da DA

Lear's famous admonition to Cordelia would look like this in terms of stressed and unstressed syllables:

~ / ~ / ~ / ~ / ~ /
Nothing will come of nothing. Speak again

The emphasis on the word "nothing" changes in the course of the line.

King Lear is approximately 3300 lines long and, of these, almost 800 are written in prose. Prose contrasts strongly with the elevated style of blank verse. In Shakespeare's plays, prose is used in letters and other documents, and usually in scenes involving servants and members of the lower classes, scenes involving madness, and scenes of comic relief. If servants are speaking nobly, however, they use verse, and if nobles are chatting informally, they may use prose.

M. VVilliam Shake-ſpeare,

HIS

True Chronicle Hiſtory of the life

and death of King *Lear*, and his
three Daughters.

With the vnfortunate life of E D G A R,
ſonne and heire to the Earle of *Gloceſter*, and
his ſullen and aſſumed humour of T O M
of Bedlam .

*As it was plaid before the Kings Maieſty at White-Hall, vp-
pon S. Stephens night, in Chriſtmas Hollidaies.*

By his Maieſties Seruants, playing vſually at the
Globe on the *Banck-ſide.*

Printed for *Nathaniel Butter.*
1608.

Title page of *King Lear* from the Second Quarto, 1619

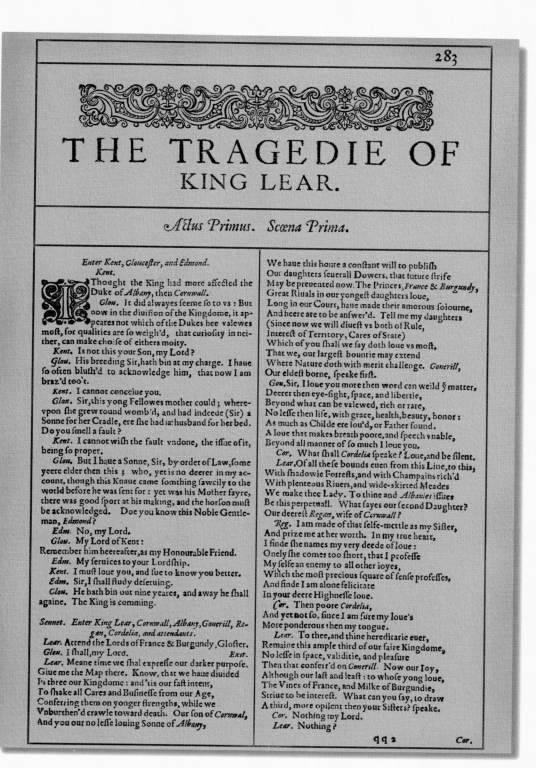

First page of *King Lear* from the First Folio, 1623

Reading Shakespeare

Did you know that in Shakespeare's day there was no rule book for grammar? There was little consistency in punctuation and spelling among writers and printing houses.

It should also be noted that Shakespeare used colons and commas to cue actors and readers where to pause and what words to emphasize.

This edition retains many of Shakespeare's original commas that we would consider unnecessary today. Use the commas to help you with your reading.

A performance at the Globe Theatre

Stage Directions

Shakespeare used stage directions very sparingly. Because he was directly involved in the production of his plays, there was little need to record the stage directions.

In this edition, the stage directions that appear in italics are Shakespeare's. Directions that are included in square brackets [ ] have been added by the editor. A long dash "—" in a speech indicates that the speaker is addressing someone other than the person to whom the actor was first speaking.

The following stage directions appear frequently in Shakespeare's plays:

Above, aloft – speech or scene played in the balcony above the stage level or from higher up in the loft

Alarum – a loud shout, a signal call to arms

Aside – spoken directly to the audience or to a specified character and not heard by the others on the stage

Below, beneath – speech or scene played from below the surface of the stage. The actor stands inside an open trap-door.

Exit – he/she leaves the stage

Exeunt – they leave the stage

Falls – the actor is wounded and falls

Flourish – fanfare of trumpets, usually announcing the entrance of royalty

Hautboys – musicians enter playing wind instruments

Manent – they remain

Omnes – all, everyone

Sennet – trumpet announcing the entrance of a procession

Severally – actors enter from, or exit in, different directions

Torchbearers – actors carry torches, a clue to the audience that the scene takes place in the dark, either at night or in an area that is not naturally lit

Within – words spoken off-stage in what the audience would assume is an unseen room, corridor, or the outdoors

THE SETTING FOR KING LEAR

IRELAND

BRITAIN

WALES

Leicester

Gloucester

Sarum Plain

CORNWALL

Salisbury

KENT
Dover

FRANCE

N

Dramatis Personae

The King and His Loyal Followers:

LEAR King of Britain
CORDELIA Lear's youngest daughter
EARL OF KENT Loyal follower of Lear
FOOL All-licensed fool

House of the Duke of Albany:

GONERIL Lear's eldest daughter
DUKE OF ALBANY Husband of Goneril
OSWALD Steward to Goneril

House of the Duke of Cornwall:

REGAN Lear's second daughter
DUKE OF CORNWALL Husband to
   Regan

House of Gloucester:

EARL OF GLOUCESTER Loyal subject
   to Lear
EDGAR Son of Gloucester
EDMUND Gloucester's illegitimate son
OLD MAN Tenant to Gloucester

Other Nobles:

KING OF FRANCE Cordelia's suitor
DUKE OF BURGUNDY Cordelia's suitor

Courtiers and Servants:

DOCTOR In Cordelia's camp
CURAN A courtier
GENTLEMAN Cordelia's attendant
SERVANTS To Cornwall
MESSENGERS

Knights and Soldiers:

KNIGHTS Attending on Lear
CAPTAIN In Edmund's employ
HERALD

*Soldiers and Officers in the French
and British armies*

Scene: Britain

Act One
Scene 1

The stateroom in King Lear's palace.

Enter Kent, Gloucester, and Edmund.
[Kent and Gloucester converse.
Edmund stands back.]

KENT: I thought the King had more affected the Duke of Albany than Cornwall.

GLOUCESTER: It did always seem so to us. But now, in the division of the kingdom, it appears not which of the Dukes he values most, for equalities are so weighed that curiosity in neither can make choice of either's moiety.

KENT: Is not this your son, my lord?

GLOUCESTER: His breeding, sir, hath been at my charge. I have so often blushed to acknowledge him that now I am brazed to it.   10

KENT: I cannot conceive you.

GLOUCESTER: Sir, this young fellow's mother could; whereupon she grew round-wombed, and had, indeed, sir, a son for her cradle ere she had a husband for her bed. Do you smell a fault?

KENT: I cannot wish the fault undone, the issue of it being so proper.

GLOUCESTER: But I have, sir, a son by order of law, some year elder than this, who yet is no dearer in my account. Though this knave came something saucily into the   20 world before he was sent for, yet was his mother fair. There was good sport at his making, and the whoreson must be acknowledged. — Do you know this noble gentleman, Edmund?

King Lear has decided to abdicate his power and divide his kingdom among his daughters. The daughter who professes the most love for him will receive the richest part of the kingdom. The two older daughters play the game, but Cordelia refuses to flatter her father and is disowned for her reluctance. Kent is banished for defending Cordelia. Despite Cordelia's loss of dowry, the King of France agrees to marry her.

1. *affected* – regard for

5 – 6. *equalities ... moiety* – Their shares (of the kingdom) have been so equally divided that even the closest scrutiny would not convince either of the Dukes to prefer the other's share.

8. *breeding* – upbringing

10. *brazed* – hardened

11. *conceive* – understand. Gloucester puns on the second meaning of this word ("become pregnant") in the next two lines.

14. *ere* – before

20. *knave* – boy or fellow; also rude servant

28. *services* – duties

31. *out* – away, perhaps abroad

Stage Direction: *sennet* – a call on a trumpet to signal an entrance or exit

Stage Direction: *coronet* – a crown, most likely intended for Cordelia.

coronet

34. *Attend* – admit (into my presence)

36. *darker* – secret

37 – 38. *divided ... kingdom* – Elizabethans would have been shocked to hear of Lear's intentions, remembering the biblical warning that "Every kingdom divided against itself is brought to desolation" (Matt. 12:25).

38. *fast* – firm

43. *publish* – announce

44. *several dowers* – Lear's daughters may be recently married and have not yet received their dowries. Or, dowers might refer to inheritances in this case.

47. *sojourn* – visits; stay

50. *interest* – legal title

52 – 53. Lear claims that his generosity will be determined not only by his natural affection as a father but also by the quality of his daughters' responses to his question.

55. *wield the matter* – express

EDMUND: No, my lord.

GLOUCESTER: My Lord of Kent. Remember him hereafter as my honourable friend.

EDMUND: My services to your lordship.

KENT: I must love you, and sue to know you better.

EDMUND: Sir, I shall study deserving.   30

GLOUCESTER: He hath been out nine years, and away he shall again.

Sound a sennet.

The King is coming.

*Enter one bearing a coronet, King Lear,
the Dukes of Albany and Cornwall, Goneril, Regan,
Cordelia, and Attendants.*

LEAR: Attend the lords of France and Burgundy, Gloucester.

GLOUCESTER: I shall, my liege.

Exeunt [Gloucester and Edmund].

LEAR: Meantime we shall express our darker purpose.
         Give me the map there. Know we have divided
         In three our kingdom, and 'tis our fast intent
         To shake all cares and business from our age,
         Conferring them on younger strengths while we   40
         Unburdened crawl toward death. Our son of Cornwall,
         And you, our no less loving son of Albany,
         We have this hour a constant will to publish
         Our daughters' several dowers, that future strife
         May be prevented now. The Princes, France and Burgundy,
         Great rivals in our youngest daughter's love,
         Long in our court have made their amorous sojourn,
         And here are to be answered. Tell me, my daughters,
         Since now we will divest us both of rule,
         Interest of territory, cares of state,   50
         Which of you shall we say doth love us most?
         That we our largest bounty may extend
         Where nature doth with merit challenge. Goneril,
         Our eldest-born, speak first.

GONERIL: Sir, I love you more than word can wield the matter;
         Dearer than eyesight, space, and liberty;
         Beyond what can be valued, rich or rare;
         No less than life, with grace, health, beauty, honour;

18

As much as child ever loved, or father found;
A love that makes breath poor, and speech unable;   60
Beyond all manner of so much I love you.

CORDELIA: [Aside.]
What shall Cordelia speak? Love, and be silent.

LEAR: Of all these bounds, even from this line to this,
With shadowy forests and with champains riched,
With plenteous rivers and wide-skirted meads,
We make thee lady. To thine and Albany's issue
Be this perpetual. — What says our second daughter,
Our dearest Regan, wife of Cornwall?

REGAN: I am made of the self metal that my sister,
And prize me at her worth. In my true heart   70
I find she names my very deed of love.
Only she comes too short, that I profess
Myself an enemy to all other joys
Which the most precious square of sense possesses,
And find I am alone felicitate
In your dear Highness' love.

CORDELIA: [Aside.]
Then poor Cordelia!
And yet not so, since I am sure my love's
More richer than my tongue.

LEAR: To thee and thine, hereditary ever,   80
Remain this ample third of our fair kingdom,
No less in space, validity, and pleasure,
Than that conferred on Goneril. — Now, our joy,
Although the last, not least, to whose young love
The vines of France and milk of Burgundy
Strive to be interested. What can you say to draw
A third more opulent than your sisters? Speak.

CORDELIA: Nothing, my lord.

LEAR: Nothing?

CORDELIA: Nothing.   90

LEAR: Nothing will come of nothing. Speak again.

CORDELIA: Unhappy that I am, I cannot heave
My heart into my mouth. I love your Majesty
According to my bond. No more nor less.

LEAR: How, how, Cordelia? Mend your speech a little,
Lest you may mar your fortunes.

CORDELIA: Good my lord,
You have begot me, bred me, loved me. I
Return those duties back as are right fit,
Obey you, love you, and most honour you.   100
Why have my sisters husbands, if they say

64. *shadowy* – shady
64. *champains riched* – fertile plains
65. *wide-skirted meads* – broad grasslands
69. *self* – same
70. *prize ... worth* – consider my love equal to hers
74. *square* – carpenter's square, used for measurement
75. *felicitate* – made happy
85. *vines* – vineyards
85. *milk* – pastures
86. *interested* – closely connected

"What Cordelia's pending marriage has forced Lear to face ... is the very human fear of crawling toward death alone, unloved, and without family. It is the desire to prevent this threat that motivates him to call together his whole family and attempt to bind to him not only the loved child who is about to depart but even the two unloved ones who have separated from him and owe primary loyalties to husbands and homes of their own."
– Lynda E. Boose, American scholar, University of California

94. *bond* – obligation as a daughter

100. *Obey ... honour you* – Shakespeare rephrases the traditional Christian marriage vow taken by a wife.

103. *plight* – pledge

113. *Hecate* – goddess of witchcraft and the underworld
114. *operation ... orbs* – influence of the stars
117. *Propinquity ... blood* – family ties; kinship
119. *Scythian* – a proverbially primitive and cruel person
120. *makes ... messes* – eats his offspring
120 – 123. Lear says he would rather befriend a Scythian than his ungrateful daughter Cordelia.
123. *sometime* – former

126. Lear, an early Celtic leader, refers to himself as a dragon. To the Celts, the dragon symbolized royalty.

130. *Who stirs?* – Lear asks why no one has responded to his commands.
136. *troop* – are associated
137. *With reservation* – Lear reserves the right to keep one hundred knights to serve him.

140. *additions to* – titles of

RELATED READING

Nothing Shall Come of Nothing – fiction by Mairi MacInnes (page 157)

They love you all? Happily, when I shall wed,
That lord whose hand must take my plight shall carry
Half my love with him, half my care and duty.
Sure I shall never marry like my sisters,
To love my father all.

LEAR: But goes thy heart with this?

CORDELIA: Ay, good my lord.

LEAR: So young, and so untender?

CORDELIA: So young, my lord, and true.   110

LEAR: Let it be so! Thy truth then be thy dower!
For, by the sacred radiance of the sun,
The mysteries of Hecate and the night,
By all the operation of the orbs
From whom we do exist and cease to be,
Here I disclaim all my paternal care,
Propinquity and property of blood,
And as a stranger to my heart and me
Hold thee from this for ever. The barbarous Scythian,
Or he that makes his generation messes   120
To gorge his appetite, shall to my bosom
Be as well neighboured, pitied, and relieved,
As thou my sometime daughter.

KENT: Good my liege —

LEAR: Peace, Kent!
Come not between the dragon and his wrath.
I loved her most, and thought to set my rest
On her kind nursery. — Hence and avoid my sight! —
So be my grave my peace, as here I give
Her father's heart from her! Call France! Who stirs?   130
Call Burgundy! Cornwall and Albany,
With my two daughters' dowers digest the third.
Let pride, which she calls plainness, marry her.
I do invest you jointly in my power,
Pre-eminence, and all the large effects
That troop with majesty. Ourself, by monthly course,
With reservation of an hundred knights,
By you to be sustained, shall our abode
Make with you by due turns. Only we shall retain
The name, and all the additions to a king. The sway,   140
Revenue, execution of the rest,
Beloved sons, be yours, which to confirm,
This coronet part between you.

KENT: Royal Lear,
Whom I have ever honoured as my King,

Loved as my father, as my master followed,
As my great patron thought on in my prayers —
LEAR: The bow is bent and drawn. Make from the shaft.
KENT: Let it fall rather, though the fork invade
    The region of my heart! Be Kent unmannerly   150
    When Lear is mad. What wouldst thou do, old man?
    Think'st thou that duty shall have dread to speak
    When power to flattery bows? To plainness honour's
        bound
    When majesty falls to folly. Reverse thy doom,
    And in thy best consideration check
    This hideous rashness. Answer my life my judgment,
    Thy youngest daughter does not love thee least,
    Nor are those empty-hearted whose low sound
    Reverbs no hollowness.
LEAR: Kent, on thy life, no more!   160
KENT: My life I never held but as a pawn
    To wage against thine enemies, nor fear to lose it,
    Thy safety being motive.
LEAR: Out of my sight!
KENT: See better, Lear, and let me still remain
    The true blank of thine eye.
LEAR: Now by Apollo —
KENT: Now by Apollo, King,
    Thou swear'st thy gods in vain.
LEAR: O vassal! Miscreant!   170

[Laying his hand on his sword.]

ALBANY:
CORNWALL: } Dear sir, forbear!
KENT: Kill thy physician, and thy fee bestow
    Upon the foul disease. Revoke thy gift,
    Or, whilst I can vent clamour from my throat,
    I'll tell thee thou dost evil.
LEAR: Hear me, recreant!
    On thine allegiance, hear me!
    Since thou hast sought to make us break our vow,
    Which we durst never yet, and with strained pride
    To come betwixt our sentence and our power,   180
    Which nor our nature nor our place can bear,
    Our potency made good, take thy reward.
    Five days we do allot thee for provision
    To shield thee from disasters of the world,

149. *fork* – arrowhead
156 – 159. *Answer ... hollowness* – Kent is willing to bet his
life that Cordelia truly loves her
father, even though her answer
seemed restrained. Most
Elizabethans would have been
familiar with the proverb that
"empty vessels have the
loudest sounds."
161. *pawn* – stake of little
value placed on a wager
166. *blank* – the white centre
of a target

"Lear's refusal to listen to
Kent's defence is made
particularly ironic when the
king calls on Apollo, the god
of light and justice. Although
he swears by Apollo, he
remains unenlightened about
the merits of his child or his
servant and so behaves
unjustly."
– Frances Teague, American
scholar, University of Georgia

170. *vassal! Miscreant!* – slave!
Villain!
174. *vent clamour* – utter
protests

"With his aggressive insis-
tence on telling Lear that he
'dost evil,' Kent fills up
Cordelia's silences."
– Martha Tuck Rozett,
American scholar, State
University of New York

176. *recreant* – traitor
179. *strained* – unnatural;
excessive
181. *nor ... nor* – neither ... nor
182. *potency ... good* – To
prove that he still has power,
Lear exiles Kent.

Act One • Scene 1

187. *trunk* – body
188. *Jupiter* – king of the gods. This play is set in pre-Christian England.

And on the sixth to turn thy hated back
Upon our kingdom. If, on the tenth day following,
Thy banished trunk be found in our dominions,
The moment is thy death. Away! By Jupiter,
This shall not be revoked.

KENT: Fare thee well, King. Since thus thou wilt appear, 190
Freedom lives hence, and banishment is here.

[To Cordelia.]

The gods to their dear shelter take thee maid,
That justly think'st and hast most rightly said!

[To Regan and Goneril.]

194. *approve* – confirm; prove true
195. *effects* – deeds

And your large speeches may your deeds approve,
That good effects may spring from words of love.
Thus Kent, O Princes, bids you all adieu.
He'll shape his old course in a country new.

Exit [Kent].
Flourish. Enter Gloucester, with France, Burgundy,
and Attendants.

> "[Cordelia] is as guilty of understating her love as [Goneril and Regan] were in overstating theirs ... In truth, Cordelia is young and unaware of how she loves her father; she merely knows that she does ... She is angered and hurt by her father's blindness to her love, which should not require an avowal. Pride partially motivates her reply."
> – Sophia B. Blaydes, American scholar, West Virginia University

GLOUCESTER: Here's France and Burgundy, my noble Lord.
LEAR: My Lord of Burgundy,
We first address toward you, who with this king 200
Hath rivalled for our daughter. What in the least
Will you require in present dower with her,
Or cease your quest of love?
BURGUNDY: Most royal Majesty,
I crave no more than hath your Highness offered,
Nor will you tender less.
LEAR: Right noble Burgundy,
When she was dear to us, we did hold her so,
But now her price is fallen. Sir, there she stands.
If aught within that little-seeming substance, 210
Or all of it, with our displeasure pieced,
And nothing more, may fitly like your Grace,
She's there, and she is yours.
BURGUNDY: I know no answer.
LEAR: Will you, with those infirmities she owes,
Unfriended, new adopted to our hate,
Dowered with our curse, and strangered with our oath,
Take her, or leave her?

206. *tender* – offer
210. *aught* – anything
210. Lear dismisses Cordelia as worthless and false.

215. *owes* – owns

BURGUNDY: Pardon me, royal Sir.
　　Election makes not up in such conditions.　　　　220
LEAR: Then leave her, sir; for, by the power that made me,
　　I tell you all her wealth.

　　　　　　　　[To France.]

　　　　　　　　　　　　　For you, great King,
　　I would not from your love make such a stray
　　To match you where I hate. Therefore beseech you
　　To avert your liking a more worthier way
　　Than on a wretch whom nature is ashamed
　　Almost to acknowledge hers.
FRANCE: This is most strange,
　　That she whom even but now was your best object,
　　The argument of your praise, balm of your age,　　　230
　　The best, the dearest, should in this trice of time
　　Commit a thing so monstrous to dismantle
　　So many folds of favour. Sure her offence
　　Must be of such unnatural degree
　　That monsters it, or your fore-vouched affection
　　Fall into taint. Which to believe of her
　　Must be a faith that reason without miracle
　　Should never plant in me.
CORDELIA: I yet beseech your Majesty,
　　If for I want that glib and oily art　　　　240
　　To speak and purpose not, since what I well intend,
　　I'll do it before I speak, that you make known
　　It is no vicious blot, murder, or foulness,
　　No unchaste action or dishonoured step,
　　That hath deprived me of your grace and favour,
　　But even for want of that for which I am richer,
　　A still-soliciting eye, and such a tongue
　　That I am glad I have not, though not to have it
　　Hath lost me in your liking.
LEAR: Better thou　　　　250
　　Hadst not been born than not to have pleased me better.
FRANCE: Is it but this? A tardiness in nature
　　Which often leaves the history unspoke
　　That it intends to do? My Lord of Burgundy,
　　What say you to the lady? Love's not love
　　When it is mingled with regards that stands
　　Aloof from the entire point. Will you have her?
　　She is herself a dowry.

220. *Election ... up* – it is impossible to choose

223. *make ... stray* – stray so far as
225. *avert* – direct

229. *best object* – dearest one
230. *argument* – subject
231. *trice* – moment
233 – 238. *Sure ... me* – France argues that either Lear must have been insincere in the past in praising Cordelia or her faults must be truly monstrous. And France cannot believe that Cordelia is detestable.

240. *want* – lack

247. *still-soliciting* – always begging

252. *tardiness in nature* – natural hesitation; reluctance to speak
253. *history* – inner life or feelings

256. *mingled ... regards* – mixed with trivial considerations (such as the amount of a dowry)

BURGUNDY: Royal King,
    Give but that portion which yourself proposed,   260
    And here I take Cordelia by the hand,
    Duchess of Burgundy.
LEAR: Nothing! I have sworn. I am firm.
BURGUNDY: I am sorry, then, you have so lost a father
    That you must lose a husband.
CORDELIA: Peace be with Burgundy!
    Since that respects and fortunes are his love,
    I shall not be his wife.
FRANCE: Fairest Cordelia, that art most rich, being poor;
    Most choice, forsaken, and most loved, despised!   270
    Thee and thy virtues here I seize upon.
    Be it lawful I take up what's cast away.
    Gods, gods! 'Tis strange that from their coldest neglect
    My love should kindle to inflamed respect.
    Thy dowerless daughter, King, thrown to my chance,
    Is Queen of us, of ours, and our fair France.
    Not all the dukes in waterish Burgundy
    Can buy this unprized precious maid of me.
    Bid them farewell, Cordelia, though unkind.
    Thou losest here, a better where to find.   280
LEAR: Thou hast her, France. Let her be thine, for we
    Have no such daughter, nor shall ever see
    That face of hers again. Therefore be gone
    Without our grace, our love, our benison.
    Come, noble Burgundy.

*Flourish. Exeunt [all but France, Goneril, Regan,
and Cordelia].*

FRANCE: Bid farewell to your sisters.
CORDELIA: The jewels of our father, with washed eyes
    Cordelia leaves you. I know you what you are,
    And like a sister, am most loath to call
    Your faults as they are named. Love well our father.   290
    To your professed bosoms I commit him.
    But yet, alas, stood I within his grace,
    I would prefer him to a better place.
    So farewell to you both.
GONERIL: Prescribe not us our duty.
REGAN: Let your study
    Be to content your lord, who hath received you
    At Fortune's alms. You have obedience scanted,
    And well are worth the want that you have wanted.

274. *respect* – affection; love

277. *waterish* – France plays on the double meaning of *waterish* — "abounding with rivers" and "weak or thinned"

280. *where* – place

284. *benison* – blessing

287. *jewels* – Regan and Goneril
287. *washed eyes* – a double meaning — tearful or having clear vision

291. *professed bosoms* – love that has been publicly announced

295. *Prescribe* – dictate; advise
298. *alms* – charity
298. *scanted* – slighted
299. "You deserve the lack of affection that you yourself failed to show."

CORDELIA: Time shall unfold what plighted cunning hides.　　　300
　　Who covers faults, at last with shame derides.
　　Well may you prosper!
FRANCE: Come, my fair Cordelia.

Exeunt France and Cordelia.

GONERIL: Sister, it is not little I have to say of what most nearly
　　appertains to us both. I think our father will hence tonight.
REGAN: That's most certain, and with you.
　　Next month with us.
GONERIL: You see how full of changes his age is. The observation
　　we have made of it hath not been little. He always loved our
　　sister most, and with what poor judgment he hath now cast　　310
　　her off appears too grossly.
REGAN: 'Tis the infirmity of his age; yet he hath ever but
　　slenderly known himself.
GONERIL: The best and soundest of his time hath been but rash.
　　Then must we look from his age, to receive not alone the
　　imperfections of long-engraffed condition, but therewithal
　　the unruly waywardness that infirm and choleric years
　　bring with them.
REGAN: Such unconstant starts are we like to have from him as
　　this of Kent's banishment.　　320
GONERIL: There is further compliment of leave-taking between
　　France and him. Pray you let us hit together. If our father
　　carry authority with such disposition as he bears, this last
　　surrender of his will but offend us.
REGAN: We shall further think of it.
GONERIL: We must do something, and in the heat.

Exeunt.

---

300. *plighted* – pleated. The metaphor suggests that Goneril and Regan are like pieces of pleated fabric — their true natures are hidden behind the folds.
301. Those who try to hide their sins will in time be scorned for their shameful faults.

311. *grossly* – obviously

313. *known himself* – been aware of his poor judgement

316. *long-engraffed* – developed over a long period of time
317. *choleric* – angry; moody

319. *unconstant* – sudden
321. *compliment* – formality
322. *hit* – agree; act
323. *carry authority* – behaves with authority
324. *surrender* – yielding of property and power
324. *offend* – cause problems
326. *in the heat* – soon (while the iron is hot)

Act One

Scene 2

The Earl of Gloucester's castle.

Enter Edmund, with a letter.

EDMUND: Thou, Nature, art my goddess. To thy law
My services are bound. Wherefore should I
Stand in the plague of custom, and permit
The curiosity of nations to deprive me,
For that I am some twelve or fourteen moonshines
Lag of a brother? Why bastard? Wherefore base?
When my dimensions are as well compact,
My mind as generous, and my shape as true,
As honest madam's issue? Why brand they us
With base? With baseness? Bastardy? Base, base?   10
Who, in the lusty stealth of nature, take
More composition and fierce quality
Than doth, within a dull, stale, tired bed,
Go to the creating a whole tribe of fops
Got 'tween asleep and wake? Well then,
Legitimate Edgar, I must have your land.
Our father's love is to the bastard Edmund
As to the legitimate. Fine word, "legitimate"!
Well, my legitimate, if this letter speed,
And my invention thrive, Edmund the base   20
Shall top the legitimate. I grow, I prosper.
Now, gods, stand up for bastards!

Enter Gloucester.

GLOUCESTER: Kent banished thus? And France in choler parted?
And the King gone tonight? Prescribed his power?
Confined to exhibition? All this done
Upon the gad? — Edmund, how now? What news?

Edmund, Gloucester's illegitimate son, tricks his father into believing that the legitimate son, Edgar, is plotting to kill Gloucester. Edmund agrees to place Gloucester where he can overhear Edgar and determine his true nature. Later, Edmund tells Edgar that he should go into hiding to escape Gloucester's anger.

1. *Thou ... goddess* – Edmund's values are materialistic rather than spiritual.
3. *plague of* – hateful; pestilent
4. *curiosity* – foolish sensibilities
5. *moonshines* – months
6. *Lag of* – behind (in age)
7. *compact* – composed; put together
11. *lusty ... nature* – secret natural lust
12. *More* – fuller
14. *fops* – dandies; weaklings

19. *speed* – succeeds
20. *invention* – plot

23. *choler* – anger
24. *Prescribed* – limited
25. *Confined to exhibition* – a university term meaning "living within the restrictions of a small allowance"
26. *gad* – whim; spur of the moment

EDMUND: So please your Lordship, none.

[Hides the letter.]

GLOUCESTER: Why so earnestly seek you to put up that letter?

EDMUND: I know no news, my Lord.

GLOUCESTER: What paper were you reading? 30

EDMUND: Nothing, my Lord.

GLOUCESTER: No? What needed then that terrible dispatch of it into your pocket? The quality of nothing hath not such need to hide itself. Let's see. Come, if it be nothing, I shall not need spectacles.

EDMUND: I beseech you, Sir, pardon me. It is a letter from my brother that I have not all over-read, and for so much as I have perused, I find it not fit for your overlooking.

GLOUCESTER: Give me the letter, sir.

EDMUND: I shall offend, either to detain or give it. The contents 40 as in part I understand them, are to blame.

GLOUCESTER: Let's see, let's see!

EDMUND: I hope, for my brother's justification, he wrote this but as an essay or taste of my virtue.

GLOUCESTER: *[Reads.] This policy and reverence of age makes the world bitter to the best of our times; keeps our fortunes from us till our oldness cannot relish them. I begin to find an idle and fond bondage in the oppression of aged tyranny, who sways, not as it hath power, but as it is suffered. Come to me, that of this I may speak more.* 50 *If our father would sleep till I waked him, you should enjoy half his revenue for ever, and live the beloved of your brother,*

Edgar.

Hum! Conspiracy! "Sleep till I waked him, you should enjoy half his revenue." My son Edgar! Had he a hand to write this? A heart and brain to breed it in? When came you to this? Who brought it?

EDMUND: It was not brought me, my Lord. There's the cunning of it. I found it thrown in at the casement of my closet. 60

GLOUCESTER: You know the character to be your brother's?

EDMUND: If the matter were good, my lord, I durst swear it were his, but in respect of that, I would fain think it were not.

GLOUCESTER: It is his.

EDMUND: It is his hand, my lord, but I hope his heart is not in the contents.

GLOUCESTER: Has he never before sounded you in this business?

33 – 34. This speech contains several echoes of Cordelia's "Nothing" in the previous scene.

41. *to blame* – blameworthy

44. *essay* – test
45. *policy ... age* – policy of respecting the old
46. *best ... times* – i.e., youth
48. *fond* – foolish
50. *suffered* – tolerated

60. *casement ... closet* – window of my chamber

63. *fain* – rather

Act One • Scene 2

71. *as ward to* – taken care of by

80. *certain* – safe

83. *pawn* – wager

84. *feel* – test

85. *pretence* – intent; purpose

87. *meet* – fitting; wise

88. *auricular* – audible

91. An individual grossly deviating from the norm would have been considered unnatural and a monster by the Elizabethans.

94 – 95. *Wind ... him* – "Win your way into his confidence for me."

96. "I would give up everything to be free of this uncertainty."

97. *convey* – conduct

99. A son plotting to kill his father would have been considered a violation of the natural order of the universe. The Elizabethans believed that nature would reflect this disorder and be thrown into chaos. This chaos would be announced through eclipses, meteor showers, violent storms, and other unnatural occurrences.

100. *wisdom of nature* – reason; common sense

102. *sequent* – following

102 – 107. *Love ... child* – Gloucester's speech refers to a biblical passage: "Take heed ... ye shall hear of wars and rumours of war ... For nation shall rise against nation, and kingdom against kingdom ... Now the brother shall betray the brother to death, and the father the son; and children shall rise up against their parents, and shall cause them to be put to death" (Mark 13:5–12).

EDMUND: Never, my lord. But I have heard him oft maintain it to be fit that, sons at perfect age, and fathers declined, the father should be as ward to the son, and the son manage his revenue. 70

GLOUCESTER: O villain, villain! His very opinion in the letter! Abhorred villain! Unnatural, detested, brutish villain! Worse than brutish! Go, sirrah, seek him. I'll apprehend him. Abominable villain! Where is he?

EDMUND: I do not well know, my lord. If it shall please you to suspend your indignation against my brother till you can derive from him better testimony of his intent, you should run a certain course. Where, if you violently 80 proceed against him, mistaking his purpose, it would make a great gap in your own honour and shake in pieces the heart of his obedience. I dare pawn down my life for him that he hath writ this to feel my affection to your honour, and to no other pretence of danger.

GLOUCESTER: Think you so?

EDMUND: If your honour judge it meet, I will place you where you shall hear us confer of this and by an auricular assurance have your satisfaction, and that without any further delay than this very evening. 90

GLOUCESTER: He cannot be such a monster.

EDMUND: Nor is not, sure.

GLOUCESTER: To his father, that so tenderly and entirely loves him. Heaven and earth! Edmund, seek him out. Wind me into him, I pray you. Frame the business after your own wisdom. I would unstate myself to be in a due resolution.

EDMUND: I will seek him, Sir, presently, convey the business as I shall find means, and acquaint you withal.

GLOUCESTER: These late eclipses in the sun and moon portend no good to us. Though the wisdom of nature can reason 100 it thus and thus, yet nature finds itself scourged by the sequent effects. Love cools, friendship falls off, brothers divide. In cities, mutinies; in countries, discord; in palaces, treason; and the bond cracked 'twixt son and father. This villain of mine comes under the prediction. There's son against father. The King falls from bias of nature. There's father against child. We have seen the best of our time. Machinations, hollowness, treachery, and all ruinous disorders follow us disquietly to our graves. Find out this villain, Edmund. It shall lose thee nothing. Do it 110 carefully. And the noble and true-hearted Kent banished! His offence, honesty! 'Tis strange.

Exit.

28

EDMUND: This is the excellent foppery of the world, that, when we are sick in fortune, often the surfeits of our own behaviour, we make guilty of our disasters the sun, the moon, and the stars. As if we were villains on necessity, fools by heavenly compulsion, knaves, thieves, and treachers by spherical predominance, drunkards, liars, and adulterers by an enforced obedience of planetary influence; and all that we are evil in, by a divine thrusting on. An admirable evasion of whoremaster man, to lay his goatish disposition to the charge of a star! My father compounded with my mother under the dragon's tail, and my nativity was under Ursa Major, so that it follows I am rough and lecherous. Fut! I should have been that I am, had the maidenliest star in the firmament twinkled on my bastardizing. Edgar —

120

Enter Edgar.

and pat, he comes, like the catastrophe of the old comedy. My cue is villainous melancholy, with a sigh like Tom o' Bedlam. — O, these eclipses do portend these divisions! Fa, sol, la, mi.

130

EDGAR: How now, brother Edmund? What serious contemplation are you in?

EDMUND: I am thinking, brother, of a prediction I read this other day, what should follow these eclipses.

EDGAR: Do you busy yourself with that?

EDMUND: I promise you, the effects he writes of succeed unhappily. As of unnaturalness between the child and the parent. Death, dearth, dissolutions of ancient amities. Divisions in state, menaces and maledictions against King and nobles. Needless diffidences, banishment of friends, dissipation of cohorts, nuptial breaches, and I know not what.

140

EDGAR: How long have you been a sectary astronomical?

EDMUND: Come, come! When saw you my father last?

EDGAR: The night gone by.

EDMUND: Spake you with him?

EDGAR: Ay, two hours together.

EDMUND: Parted you in good terms? Found you no displeasure in him by word nor countenance?

150

EDGAR: None at all.

EDMUND: Bethink yourself wherein you may have offended him; and at my entreaty forbear his presence until some little time hath qualified the heat of his displeasure,

106 – 107. *falls ... nature* – fails to act according to natural inclination
113. *foppery* – folly
114. *surfeits* – excesses
115. *make guilty of* – blame. Edmund scoffs at those who blame the stars for their own faults or poor fortune. Many people today would agree with his view. In Shakespeare's day, however, Edmund's speech would condemn him as a cynic and an atheist.
118. *treachers* – traitors
122. *lay* – blame
124. *dragon's tail* – the constellation Draco
124. *Ursa Major* – the constellation Great Bear
128. *catastrophe* – conclusion
130. *Tom o' Bedlam* – a common name for a beggar who is thought to be insane. Bedlam comes from the Hospital of St. Mary of Bethlehem, the name of an insane asylum in London.

139. *amities* – friendships; alliances
141. *diffidences* – distrust
142. *dissipation of cohorts* – breaking up of armies
144. *sectary astronomical* – follower of astrology

153. *forbear* – avoid
154. *qualified* – reduced; moderated

158 – 159. *have ...*
forbearance – remain calm
and keep out of sight

165. *meaning* – intention
166. *faintly* – in an
understated way
167. *image and horror* –
horrible reality
168. *anon* – soon

170. *credulous* – gullible
173. *practices* – schemes
174. *wit* – intelligence
175. "I will do anything
fitting and necessary to
accomplish my purposes."

which at this instant so rageth in him that with the
mischief of your person it would scarcely allay.

EDGAR: Some villain hath done me wrong.

EDMUND: That's my fear. I pray you have a continent forbearance till the speed of his rage goes slower, and as I
say, retire with me to my lodging, from whence I will   160
fitly bring you to hear my Lord speak. Pray ye, go!
There's my key. If you do stir abroad, go armed.

EDGAR: Armed, brother?

EDMUND: Brother, I advise you to the best. Go armed. I am
no honest man if there be any good meaning toward you.
I have told you what I have seen and heard. But faintly,
nothing like the image and horror of it. Pray you, away!

EDGAR: Shall I hear from you anon?

EDMUND: I do serve you in this business.

Exit Edgar.

A credulous father, and a brother noble,   170
Whose nature is so far from doing harms
That he suspects none. On whose foolish honesty
My practices ride easy! I see the business.
Let me, if not by birth, have lands by wit.
All with me's meet that I can fashion fit.

Exit.

Act One
Scene 3

A room in the Duke of Albany's palace.

Enter Goneril and Oswald, her Steward.

GONERIL: Did my father strike my gentleman for chiding of
his Fool?
OSWALD: Ay, madam.
GONERIL: By day and night, he wrongs me! Every hour
He flashes into one gross crime or other
That sets us all at odds. I'll not endure it.
His knights grow riotous, and himself upbraids us
On every trifle. When he returns from hunting,
I will not speak with him. Say I am sick.
If you come slack of former services,   10
You shall do well. The fault of it I'll answer.
OSWALD: He's coming, madam. I hear him.

[Horns within.]

GONERIL: Put on what weary negligence you please,
You and your fellows. I'd have it come to question.
If he distaste it, let him to our sister,
Whose mind and mine, I know, in that are one,
Not to be overruled. Idle old man,
That still would manage those authorities
That he hath given away! Now, by my life,
Old fools are babes again, and must be used   20
With checks as flatteries, when they are seen abused.
Remember what I have said.
OSWALD: Very well, madam.

1. *chiding of* – rebuking

10. *slack* – short

15. *distaste* – disapproves of

17. *Idle* – foolish

20 – 21. *must ... abused* – must be controlled with rebukes when kind treatment feeds their delusions

26. *breed* – create
26. *occasions* – opportunities
27. *straight* – immediately

GONERIL: And let his knights have colder looks among you.
What grows of it, no matter. Advise your fellows so.
I would breed from hence occasions, and I shall,
That I may speak. I'll write straight to my sister
To hold my very course. Prepare for dinner.

Exeunt.

Act One
Scene 4

A hall in the Duke of Albany's palace.

Enter Kent, disguised.

KENT: If but as well I other accents borrow,
That can my speech defuse, my good intent
May carry through itself to that full issue
For which I razed my likeness. Now, banished Kent,
If thou canst serve where thou dost stand condemned,
So may it come, thy master, whom thou lov'st,
Shall find thee full of labours.

Horns within. Enter Lear, Knights, and Attendants.

LEAR: Let me not stay a jot for dinner. Go get it ready.

[Exit an Attendant.]

How now? What art thou?
KENT: A man, sir.   10
LEAR: What dost thou profess? What wouldst thou with us?
KENT: I do profess to be no less than I seem, to serve him
truly that will put me in trust, to love him that is honest,
to converse with him that is wise and says little, to fear
judgment, to fight when I cannot choose, and to eat no
fish.
LEAR: What art thou?
KENT: A very honest-hearted fellow, and as poor as the King.
LEAR: If thou be'st as poor for a subject as he is for a King,
thou art poor enough. What wouldst thou?   20

2. *defuse* – disguise. Kent appears disguised and adopts an accent.
4. *razed* – erased (through a disguise). In some contexts, this means shaved. It is unlikely, however, that a man of Kent's standing would shave his face. There is evidence later in the play (Act Two, Scene 2, line 58) that Kent still has his beard.
8. *stay* – wait

11. *profess* – work at (i.e., What is your trade?)

15 – 16. *eat no fish* – "I am a good Protestant"; or "I am strong because I eat meat."

KENT: Service.

LEAR: Who wouldst thou serve?

KENT: You.

LEAR: Dost thou know me, fellow?

KENT: No, sir; but you have that in your countenance which I would fain call master.

LEAR: What's that?

KENT: Authority.

LEAR: What services canst thou do?

KENT: I can keep honest counsel, ride, run, mar a curious tale in telling it and deliver a plain message bluntly. That which ordinary men are fit for, I am qualified in, and the best of me is diligence.

LEAR: How old art thou?

KENT: Not so young, sir, to love a woman for singing, nor so old to dote on her for anything. I have years on my back forty-eight.

LEAR: Follow me. Thou shalt serve me. If I like thee no worse after dinner, I will not part from thee yet. Dinner, ho, dinner! Where's my knave? My Fool? Go you and call my Fool hither.

[Exit an Attendant.]
Enter Oswald.

You, you, sirrah, where's my daughter?

OSWALD: So please you —

Exit [Oswald].

LEAR: What says the fellow there? Call the clotpoll back.

[Exit a Knight.]

Where's my Fool, ho? I think the world's asleep.

[Enter Knight.]

How now? Where's that mongrel?

KNIGHT: He says, my Lord, your daughter is not well.

LEAR: Why came not the slave back to me when I called him?

KNIGHT: Sir, he answered me in the roundest manner, he would not.

LEAR: He would not?

---

25. *countenance* – bearing

30. *curious* – complex; elegant — 30

44. *clotpoll* – dolt; blockhead

49. *roundest* – rudest

40

50

KNIGHT: My lord, I know not what the matter is. But to my judgment your Highness is not entertained with that ceremonious affection as you were wont. There's a great abatement of kindness appears as well in the general dependants as in the Duke himself also and your daughter.

LEAR: Ha! Say'st thou so?

KNIGHT: I beseech you pardon me, my lord, if I be mistaken, for my duty cannot be silent when I think your Highness wronged.   60

LEAR: Thou but rememb'rest me of mine own conception. I have perceived a most faint neglect of late, which I have rather blamed as mine own jealous curiosity than as a very pretence and purpose of unkindness. I will look further into it. But where's my Fool? I have not seen him this two days.

KNIGHT: Since my young Lady's going into France, sir, the Fool hath much pined away.

LEAR: No more of that. I have noted it well. Go you, and tell   70
my daughter I would speak with her.

[Exit Knight.]

Go you, call hither my Fool.

[Exit an Attendant.] Enter Oswald.

O, you, sir, you! Come you hither, sir.
Who am I, sir?

OSWALD: My Lady's father.

LEAR: "My Lady's father!" My Lord's knave! You whoreson dog! You slave! You cur!

OSWALD: I am none of these, my Lord. I beseech your pardon.

LEAR: Do you bandy looks with me, you rascal?

[Strikes him.]

OSWALD: I'll not be strucken, my lord.   80

KENT: Nor tripped neither, you base football player.

[Trips up his heels.]

LEAR: I thank thee, fellow. Thou serv'st me, and I'll love thee.

53. *entertained* – treated

55. *abatement* – lessening
56. *dependants* – servants

62. *rememb'rest* – reminded
62. *conception* – idea
64. *jealous* – suspicious
65. *very pretence* – true intention

79. *bandy* – exchange

81. *football* – a sport similar to today's soccer. In Shakespeare's day, football was scorned. In his treatise on educational politics, Sir Thomas Elyot (1490–1546) described it as a game to be avoided by "all noble men … wherein is nothing but beastly fury and extreme violence."

football

83. *differences* – the difference between a servant and a king
84. "If you wish to be tripped again"
85. *tarry* – stay
86. *earnest* – payment in advance of a larger reward
88. *coxcomb* – the cap of a jester, decorated to resemble the comb of a rooster.

coxcomb

92 – 94. *Nay ... shortly* – "If you don't support the party with the power, you will be turned out of doors soon."
97. *Nuncle* – a contraction for "mine uncle"
100. *living* – possessions
103 – 104. "Telling the truth is punishable, while flattery is rewarded."
104. *Lady Brach* – a common name for a dog
105. *gall* – irritation

111. *owest* – own
112. *goest* – walk
113. "Do not believe everything you hear."
114. "Do not bet everything on a single throw of the dice."
118. *score* – twenty

KENT: Come, sir, arise, away! I'll teach you differences. Away, away! If you will measure your lubber's length again, tarry, but away! Go to! Have you wisdom? So.

[Pushes Oswald out.]

LEAR: Now, my friendly knave, I thank thee. There's earnest of thy service.

[Gives Kent money.] Enter Fool.

FOOL: Let me hire him too. Here's my coxcomb.

[Offers Kent his cap.]

LEAR: How now, my pretty knave? How dost thou?
FOOL: Sirrah, you were best take my coxcomb.   90
KENT: Why, fool?
FOOL: Why? For taking one's part that's out of favour. Nay, an thou canst not smile as the wind sits, thou'lt catch cold shortly. There, take my coxcomb! Why, this fellow hath banished two on's daughters, and did the third a blessing against his will. If thou follow him, thou must needs wear my coxcomb. — How now, Nuncle? Would I had two coxcombs and two daughters!
LEAR: Why, my boy?
FOOL: If I gave them all my living, I'd keep my coxcombs   100 myself. There's mine. Beg another of thy daughters.
LEAR: Take heed, sirrah, the whip.
FOOL: Truth's a dog must to kennel. He must be whipped out, when the Lady Brach may stand by the fire and stink.
LEAR: A pestilent gall to me!
FOOL: Sirrah, I'll teach thee a speech.
LEAR: Do.
FOOL: Mark it, Nuncle.
        Have more than thou showest,
        Speak less than thou knowest,   110
        Lend less than thou owest,
        Ride more than thou goest,
        Learn more than thou trowest,
        Set less than thou throwest.
        Leave thy drink and thy whore,
        And keep in-a-door,
        And thou shalt have more
        Than two tens to a score.

KENT: This is nothing, Fool.

FOOL: Then 'tis like the breath of an unfee'd lawyer — you 120
gave me nothing for it. Can you make no use of nothing,
Nuncle?

LEAR: Why, no, boy. Nothing can be made out of nothing.

FOOL: *[To Kent.]*
Prithee tell him, so much the rent of his land comes to.
He will not believe a Fool.

LEAR: A bitter Fool!

FOOL: Dost thou know the difference, my boy, between a
bitter Fool and a sweet one?

LEAR: No, lad. Teach me.

FOOL: That lord that counselled thee 130
To give away thy land,
Come place him here by me,
Do thou for him stand.
The sweet and bitter fool
Will presently appear;
The one in motley here,
The other found out there.

LEAR: Dost thou call me fool, boy?

FOOL: All thy other titles thou hast given away, that thou
wast born with. 140

KENT: This is not altogether fool, my lord.

FOOL: No, faith, lords and great men will not let me. If I had
a monopoly out, they would have part on it. And ladies
too, they will not let me have all the fool to myself.
They'll be snatching. Nuncle, give me an egg, and I'll
give thee two crowns.

LEAR: What two crowns shall they be?

FOOL: Why, after I have cut the egg in the middle and eat up
the meat, the two crowns of the egg. When thou clovest
thy crown in the middle and gav'st away both parts, thou 150
bor'st thine ass on thy back over the dirt. Thou hadst
little wit in thy bald crown when thou gav'st thy golden
one away. If I speak like myself in this, let him be
whipped that first finds it so.

[Sings.] Fools had never less grace in a year,
For wise men are grown foppish,
And know not how their wits to wear,
Their manners are so apish.

LEAR: When were you wont to be so full of songs, sirrah?

120. *breath* – words
121. *nothing* – Here are further echoes of Cordelia's "Nothing."

133. *stand* – pretend to be
136. *motley* – the patchwork costume of the professional fool

motley

142. *let me* – allow me to be (the only fool)

151. *bor'st thine ass* – carried your donkey

156. *foppish* – foolish

158. *apish* – ridiculous

Act One • Scene 4

160. *used it* – taken up the activity

165. *bo-peep* – a game similar to hide-and-seek

169. *And* – if

175. *pared* – cut; peeled

177. *frontlet* – frown

180. *an O ... figure* – a zero with no number in front of it

187. *shealed peascod* – shelled (empty) pea pod
188. *all-licensed* – protected; privileged. He can say anything without fear of punishment.
189. *retinue* – followers
190. *carp* – criticize

FOOL: I have used it, Nuncle, ever since thou mad'st thy   160
daughters thy mother. For when thou gav'st them the
rod, and put'st down thine own breeches,

> [*Sings.*] Then they for sudden joy did weep,
>   And I for sorrow sung,
> That such a king should play bo-peep
>   And go the fools among.

Prithee, Nuncle, keep a schoolmaster that can teach thy
Fool to lie. I would fain learn to lie.
LEAR: And you lie, sirrah, we'll have you whipped.
FOOL: I marvel what kin thou and thy daughters are. They'll   170
have me whipped for speaking true, thou'lt have me
whipped for lying, and sometimes I am whipped for
holding my peace. I had rather be any kind of thing than
a fool! And yet I would not be thee, Nuncle. Thou hast
pared thy wit on both sides and left nothing in the
middle. Here comes one of the parings.

Enter Goneril.

LEAR: How now, daughter? What makes that frontlet on?
Methinks you are too much of late in the frown.
FOOL: Thou wast a pretty fellow when thou hadst no need to
care for her frowning. Now thou art an O without a figure.   180
I am better than thou art now. I am a Fool, thou art nothing.

[To Goneril.]

Yes, forsooth, I will hold my tongue. So your face bids
me, though you say nothing.

> Mum, mum!
> He that keeps nor crust nor crum,
> Weary of all, shall want some.

[Points at Lear.]

That's a shealed peascod.
GONERIL: Not only, Sir, this your all-licensed Fool,
But other of your insolent retinue
Do hourly carp and quarrel, breaking forth   190
In rank and not-to-be-endured riots. Sir,
I had thought, by making this well known unto you,

To have found a safe redress, but now grow fearful,
By what yourself too late have spoke and done,
That you protect this course, and put it on
By your allowance. Which if you should, the fault
Would not scape censure, nor the redresses sleep,
Which, in the tender of a wholesome weal,
Might in their working do you that offence,
Which else were shame, that then necessity   200
Will call discreet proceeding.

FOOL: For you know, Nuncle,

      The hedge-sparrow fed the cuckoo so long,
      That it's had it head bit off by it young.

So out went the candle, and we were left darkling.
LEAR: Are you our daughter?
GONERIL: Come, sir,
I would you would make use of that good wisdom
Whereof I know you are fraught, and put away
These dispositions that of late transform you   210
From what you rightly are.
FOOL: May not an ass know when the cart draws the horse?
Whoop, Jug, I love thee!
LEAR: Does any here know me?
This is not Lear.
Does Lear walk thus? Speak thus? Where are his eyes?
Either his notion weakens, his discernings
Are lethargied — Ha! Waking? 'Tis not so.
Who is it that can tell me who I am?
FOOL: Lear's shadow.   220
LEAR: I would learn that, for by the marks of sovereignty,
knowledge, and reason, I should be false persuaded
I had daughters.
FOOL: Which they will make an obedient father.
LEAR: Your name, fair gentlewoman?
GONERIL: This admiration, Sir, is much of the savour
Of other your new pranks. I do beseech you
To understand my purposes aright.
As you are old and reverend, you should be wise.
Here do you keep a hundred knights and squires.   230
Men so disordered, so debauched, and bold
That this our court, infected with their manners,
Shows like a riotous inn. Epicurism and lust
Make it more like a tavern or a brothel
Than a graced palace. The shame itself doth speak

195 – 196. *put ... allowance* – encourage it by implicit approval

196 – 201. "Which if you do, you will not escape criticism, and although you might be offended by my disciplinary actions, they are clearly necessary to maintain an orderly household."

205. *darkling* – in the dark

209. *fraught* – furnished

212. The Fool's jest about the cart pulling the horse is meant to show how ridiculous it is for a daughter to give commands to her father and King.

"May not an ass know when the cart draws the horse?"

217. *notion* – reasoning powers
218. *lethargied* – drugged; asleep
226. *admiration* – wonderment
233. *Epicurism* – a philosophy that gives rise to gluttony
235. *graced* – stately; royal

236. *desired* – requested
237. *else* – otherwise
238. *disquantity* – reduce the number of
240. *besort* – suit

For instant remedy. Be then desired
By her that else will take the thing she begs
A little to disquantity your train,
And the remainder that shall still depend
To be such men as may besort your age,   240
Which know themselves and you.
LEAR: Darkness and devils!
Saddle my horses! Call my train together!
Degenerate bastard, I'll not trouble thee.
Yet have I left a daughter.
GONERIL: You strike my people, and your disordered
rabble make servants of their betters.

Enter Albany.

LEAR: Woe that too late repents! — O, sir, are you come?
Is it your will? Speak, sir! — Prepare my horses. —
Ingratitude, thou marble-hearted fiend,   250
More hideous when thou show'st thee in a child
Than the sea-monster!
ALBANY: Pray, sir, be patient.
LEAR: *[To Goneril.]* Detested kite, thou liest!
My train are men of choice and rarest parts,
That all particulars of duty know
And in the most exact regard support
The worships of their name. — O most small fault,
How ugly didst thou in Cordelia show!
Which, like an engine, wrenched my frame of nature   260
From the fixed place, drew from my heart all love,
And added to the gall. O Lear, Lear, Lear!
Beat at this gate that let thy folly in

[Strikes at his head.]

And thy dear judgment out! Go, go, my people.
ALBANY: My lord, I am guiltless, as I am ignorant
Of what hath moved you.
LEAR: It may be so, my Lord.
Hear, Nature, hear! Dear goddess, hear!
Suspend thy purpose, if thou didst intend
To make this creature fruitful.   270
Into her womb convey sterility!
Dry up in her the organs of increase,
And from her derogate body never spring
A babe to honour her! If she must teem,

254. *kite* – bird of prey

kite

262. *gall* – bitterness

266. *moved* – angered

273. *derogate* – degraded
274. *teem* – be fruitful; i.e., have children

Create her child of spleen, that it may live
And be a thwart disnatured torment to her.
Let it stamp wrinkles in her brow of youth,
With cadent tears fret channels in her cheeks,
Turn all her mother's pains and benefits
To laughter and contempt, that she may feel   280
How sharper than a serpent's tooth it is
To have a thankless child! Away, away!

Exit.

ALBANY: Now, gods that we adore, whereof comes this?
GONERIL: Never afflict yourself to know the cause;
    But let his disposition have that scope
    As dotage gives it.

Enter Lear.

LEAR: What, fifty of my followers at a clap?
    Within a fortnight?
ALBANY: What's the matter, sir?
LEAR: I'll tell thee.

[To Goneril.]

               Life and death! I am ashamed   290
That thou hast power to shake my manhood thus,
That these hot tears, which break from me perforce,
Should make thee worth them. Blasts and fogs upon thee!
The untented woundings of a father's curse
Pierce every sense about thee! Old fond eyes,
Beweep this cause again, I'll pluck ye out,
And cast you, with the waters that you loose,
To temper clay. Yea, is it come to this?
Ha! Let it be so. I have another daughter,
Who I am sure is kind and comfortable.   300
When she shall hear this of thee, with her nails
She'll flay thy wolvish visage. Thou shalt find
That I'll resume the shape which thou dost think
I have cast off for ever.

[Exeunt Lear, Kent, and Attendants.]

GONERIL: Do you mark that, my lord?
ALBANY: I cannot be so partial, Goneril,
    To the great love I bear you —

---

275. *spleen* – malice; spite
276. *thwart disnatured* – perverse and without natural affection
278. *cadent* – falling
278. *fret* – erode

284. *afflict* – concern

294. *untented* – too deep to be bandaged

297. *loose* – discharge
298. *temper* – soften

302. *flay* – skin; tear
302. *visage* – face; appearance

41

310. *tarry* – wait

313. *sure* – certainly be sent

314. *halter* – hangman's rope

316. *This ... counsel* – Goneril claims that the Fool would not have been so insulting if he had not been encouraged by Lear.

318. *At point* – armed

319. *buzz* – whisper

320. *enguard* – protect

321. *in mercy* – at his mercy

324. *still* – always

GONERIL: Pray you, content. — What, Oswald, ho!

[To the Fool.]

You, sir, more knave than fool, after your master!

FOOL: Nuncle Lear, Nuncle Lear, tarry! Take the Fool with thee.

A fox, when one has caught her,
And such a daughter,
Should sure to the slaughter,
If my cap would buy a halter.
So the fool follows after.

Exit.

GONERIL: This man hath had good counsel! A hundred nights?
'Tis politic and safe to let him keep
At point a hundred knights. Yes, that on every dream,
Each buzz, each fancy, each complaint, dislike,
He may enguard his dotage with their powers
And hold our lives in mercy. — Oswald, I say!

ALBANY: Well, you may fear too far.

GONERIL: Safer than trust too far.
Let me still take away the harms I fear,
Not fear still to be taken. I know his heart.
What he hath uttered I have writ my sister.
If she sustain him and his hundred knights,
When I have showed the unfitness —

Enter [Oswald the] Steward.

How now, Oswald?
What, have you writ that letter to my sister?   330
OSWALD: Yes, madam.
GONERIL: Take you some company, and away to horse!
   Inform her full of my particular fear,
   And thereto add such reasons of your own
   As may compact it more. Get you gone,
   And hasten your return.

[Exit Oswald.]

No, no, my lord!
This milky gentleness and course of yours,
Though I condemn not, yet, under pardon,
You are much more at task for want of wisdom
Than praised for harmful mildness.   340
ALBANY: How far your eyes may pierce I cannot tell.
   Striving to better, oft we mar what's well.
GONERIL: Nay then —
ALBANY: Well, well, the event.

Exeunt.

335. *compact* – confirm

337. *milky* – affectionate

339. *at task* – taken to task
340. *harmful mildness* – softness that proves harmful

344. *Well ... event* – "We will see what happens."

"The world in which the tragedy of *King Lear* takes place is vague and dark. The locations of Lear's castle and the castles of Albany and Cornwall are not made clear. Nor is it clear how so many messengers can be sent simultaneously to the same places, arrive at their destinations only seconds apart, and never meet on the way."
– Harriet Dye, American scholar

Act One
Scene 5

Lear sends Kent ahead with letters for Regan. Lear and the Fool banter with each other before setting off themselves for Regan's.

3. *demand* – questions
7. *kibes* – inflammations caused by cold
10. *slip-shod* – slippered
13. *she's* – Regan is
13. *this* – Goneril
13. *crab* – crab apple

"The subject of *Lear* is renunciation, and it is only by being wilfully blind that one can fail to understand what Shakespeare is saying. Lear renounces his throne but expects everyone to continue treating him as a king. He does not see that if he surrenders power, other people will take advantage of his weakness; also that those who flatter him the most grossly, are exactly the ones who will turn against him."
– George Orwell (1903–1950), English novelist, essayist, and critic

RELATED READING

Refrain – poem by Mary Jo Salter (page 166)

A courtyard before the Duke of Albany's palace.

Enter Lear, Kent, and Fool.

LEAR: Go you before to Gloucester with these letters. Acquaint my daughter no further with anything you know than comes from her demand out of the letter. If your diligence be not speedy, I shall be there afore you.

KENT: I will not sleep, my lord, till I have delivered your letter.

Exit.

FOOL: If a man's brains were in his heels, were it not in danger of kibes?

LEAR: Ay, boy.

FOOL: Then I prithee be merry. Thy wit shall never go slip-shod.   10

LEAR: Ha, ha, ha!

FOOL: Shalt see thy other daughter will use thee kindly. For though she's as like this as a crab's like an apple, yet I can tell what I can tell.

LEAR: What canst tell, boy?

FOOL: She'll taste as like this as a crab does to a crab. Thou canst tell why one's nose stands in the middle on his face?

LEAR: No.

FOOL: Why, to keep one's eyes of either side his nose, that   20 what a man cannot smell out, he may spy into.

LEAR: I did her wrong.

FOOL: Canst tell how an oyster makes his shell?

LEAR: No.

FOOL: Nor I neither. But I can tell why a snail has a house.

LEAR: Why?

FOOL: Why, to put's head in. Not to give it away to his daughters, and leave his horns without a case.

LEAR: I will forget my nature. So kind a father! — Be my horses ready?   30

FOOL: Thy asses are gone about 'em. The reason why the seven stars are no more than seven is a pretty reason.

LEAR: Because they are not eight?

FOOL: Yes indeed. Thou wouldst make a good Fool.

LEAR: To take it again perforce! Monster ingratitude!

FOOL: If thou wert my Fool, Nuncle, I'd have thee beaten for being old before thy time.

LEAR: How's that?

FOOL: Thou shouldst not have been old till thou hadst been wise.

LEAR: O, let me not be mad, not mad, sweet heaven!   40
Keep me in temper. I would not be mad!

Enter Gentleman.

How now? Are the horses ready?

GENTLEMAN: Ready, my lord.

LEAR: Come, boy.

FOOL: She that's a maid now, and laughs at my departure,
Shall not be a maid long, unless things be cut shorter.

Exeunt.

ે ે ે

35. *To ... perforce* – Perhaps Lear is thinking about reclaiming his title and power.

41. *in temper* – sane; in control

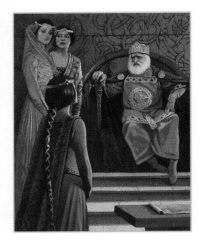

Act One Considerations

ACT ONE Scene 1

▶ The play opens with a short scene in which Gloucester and Kent discuss two different fathers' love for their children. How does Lear feel about his two older daughters? How does Gloucester feel about his two sons?

What are your first impressions of Gloucester, Kent, Cordelia, and Lear?

▶ In groups of four, create a number of newspaper articles, columns, editorials, and editorial cartoons about the events of the first scene. Lay out your articles on poster paper so that they resemble a newspaper spread.

▶ A monarch dividing up his or her kingdom would have been disturbing to the Elizabethans. Why might such a course of action be dangerous for a nation? What might be the personal consequences for the monarch and the potential heirs?

In a paragraph, discuss why elderly parents might not be inclined to divide their property, before their deaths, among their children.

▶ Summarize the evidence that suggests that Lear loves Cordelia more than his other daughters. What positive character traits does Cordelia exhibit? Is Lear justified in his treatment of Cordelia in this scene?

▶ Looking at Goneril and Regan's conversation which ends the scene, how might you expect them to treat Lear in subsequent scenes? Why?

ACT ONE Scene 2

▶ Express Edmund's opening soliloquy in modern speech. (Capture the essence of his argument rather than translating it word for word.) What do you think of the point of view he expresses in the first fifteen lines? Is his reasoning logical?

▶ Write a soliloquy for Gloucester to speak after his conversation with Edmund. Gloucester should express his thoughts and feelings about Edmund's news and explain why he believes what Edmund says. Write in prose or iambic pentameter verse (see Shakespeare's Verse and Prose on page 9).

ACT ONE Scene 3

▶ Write the letter that Goneril says she will send to her sister. The letter should describe what Goneril has endured from her father and his riotous knights. Since Shakespeare does not include many specific details, create some to make the letter sound realistic.

ACT ONE Scene 4

▶ Imagine you have been asked to hire someone to serve Lear. Write a help-wanted advertisement that would appear in the careers section of the newspaper. Using as many of Kent's words as you like, include a job description plus the qualifications and personal characteristics required of the applicant.

▶ Read "Wise Enough to Play the Fool" on page 161. To what extent does Lear's Fool exemplify the role of the court jester outlined by Asimov? Write a short paragraph in which you explore why anyone, especially a powerful person such as a king, would tolerate the activities of an "all-licensed fool."

▶ In groups, debate the following resolution: Be it resolved that Lear is justified in cursing Goneril (lines 268–282).

▶ Compile a list of all the references to eyes, eyesight, and blindings in this scene. Based on these references, what do you predict might happen later in the play?

▶ Create a two-column chart on a blank piece of paper. Label one column Good and the other one Bad. Use this chart to show which characters you think are just and admirable and which are unjust and detestable. Deal only with the major characters: Lear, his daughters and their husbands, Gloucester and his sons, Kent, Oswald, and the Fool. Compare your chart with those of your classmates and discuss any differences of opinion.

ACT ONE Scene 5

▶ Lear is over eighty years old. Goneril suggests his senses are failing. Other details indicate that Lear is still strong: for example, he still hunts and has a good appetite. If you were directing this scene, how would you present Lear? Justify your decision.

▶ From what you have seen so far in the play, what do you think is the main dramatic purpose of the Fool? Why does Lear keep the Fool close to him and why does he permit the Fool to speak to him in a way no other person can? Write a paragraph describing their relationship.

Act Two
Scene 1

The Earl of Gloucester's castle.

Enter Edmund and Curan, meeting.

EDMUND: Save thee, Curan.
CURAN: And you, sir. I have been with your father, and given
    him notice that the Duke of Cornwall and Regan his
    Duchess will be here with him this night.
EDMUND: How comes that?
CURAN: Nay, I know not. You have heard of the news abroad?
    I mean the whispered ones, for they are yet but ear-
    kissing arguments?
EDMUND: Not I. Pray you, what are they?
CURAN: Have you heard of no likely wars toward, 'twixt the   10
    Dukes of Cornwall and Albany?
EDMUND: Not a word.
CURAN: You may do, then, in time. Fare you well, sir.

Exit.

EDMUND: The Duke be here tonight? The better! Best!
    This weaves itself perforce into my business.
    My father hath set guard to take my brother;
    And I have one thing, of a queasy question,
    Which I must act. Briefness and Fortune, work!
    Brother, a word! Descend! Brother, I say!

Enter Edgar.

My father watches. O sir, fly this place!   20
Intelligence is given where you are hid.

1. *Save thee* – God save thee (a common greeting)

8. *ear-kissing arguments* – news whispered in secret
10. *toward* – impending

14. *The better* – so much the better

17. *queasy question* – sensitive matter

Edmund, carrying out his plot, persuades Edgar to flee from their father's house. Convinced of Edgar's treachery, Gloucester declares that Edmund will be his heir. Cornwall and Regan arrive and support Gloucester in his efforts to capture Edgar. Edmund joins the service of Cornwall and Regan.

You have now the good advantage of the night.
Have you not spoken 'gainst the Duke of Cornwall?
He's coming hither, now, in the night, in the haste,
And Regan with him. Have you nothing said
Upon his party 'gainst the Duke of Albany?
Advise yourself.

EDGAR: I am sure on it, not a word.

EDMUND: I hear my father coming. Pardon me!
In cunning I must draw my sword upon you.   30
Draw, seem to defend yourself. Now quit you well. —
Yield! Come before my father. Light, ho, here! —
Fly, brother. — Torches, torches! — So farewell.

Exit Edgar.

Some blood drawn on me would beget opinion

[Wounds his arm.]

Of my more fierce endeavour. I have seen drunkards
Do more than this in sport. — Father, father! —
Stop, stop! No help?

Enter Gloucester,
and Servants with torches.

GLOUCESTER: Now, Edmund, where's the villain?

EDMUND: Here stood he in the dark, his sharp sword out,
Mumbling of wicked charms, conjuring the moon   40
To stand auspicious mistress.

GLOUCESTER: But where is he?

EDMUND: Look, Sir, I bleed.

GLOUCESTER: Where is the villain, Edmund?

EDMUND: Fled this way, Sir. When by no means he could —

GLOUCESTER: Pursue him, ho! Go after.

[Exeunt some Servants.]

"By no means" what?

EDMUND: Persuade me to the murder of your lordship.
But that I told him the revenging gods
'Gainst parricides did all their thunders bend;   50
Spoke with how manifold and strong a bond

---

30. *In cunning* – to avoid appearing as friends
31. *seem* – pretend
31. *quit* – fight

34 – 35. Edmund believes that if he is seen to be bleeding, people will believe that he was engaged in a fierce battle.

41. *stand* – serve as his

50. *parricides* – murder of fathers

The child was bound to the father. Sir, in fine,
Seeing how loathly opposite I stood
To his unnatural purpose, in fell motion
With his prepared sword he charges home
My unprovided body, lanched mine arm.
But when he saw my best alarumed spirits,
Bold in the quarrel's right, roused to the encounter,
Or whether gasted by the noise I made,
Full suddenly he fled.   60
GLOUCESTER: Let him fly far.
Not in this land shall he remain uncaught.
And found — dispatch. The noble Duke my master,
My worthy arch and patron, comes tonight.
By his authority I will proclaim it,
That he which finds, him shall deserve our thanks,
Bringing the murderous coward to the stake.
He that conceals him, death.
EDMUND: When I dissuaded him from his intent
And found him pight to do it, with curst speech   70
I threatened to discover him. He replied,
"Thou unpossessing bastard! Dost thou think,
If I would stand against thee, would the reposal
Of any trust, virtue, or worth in thee
Make thy words faithed? No. What I should deny
(As this I would, ay, though thou didst produce
My very character), I'd turn it all
To thy suggestion, plot, and damned practice.
And thou must make a dullard of the world,
If they not thought the profits of my death   80
Were very pregnant and potential spirits
To make thee seek it."
GLOUCESTER: O strange and fastened villain!
Would he deny his letter? I never got him.

Tucket within.

Hark, the Duke's trumpets! I know not why he comes.
All ports I'll bar. The villain shall not scape.
The Duke must grant me that. Besides, his picture
I will send far and near, that all the kingdom
May have due note of him, and of my land,
Loyal and natural boy, I'll work the means   90
To make thee capable.

52. *in fine* – in conclusion

54. *fell* – cruel; deadly
56. *unprovided* – unprotected
56. *lanched* – lanced; wounded
57. *alarumed spirits* – awakened effort or energy
59. *gasted* – frightened

64. *arch and patron* – chief patron

70. *pight* – determined
71. *discover* – expose

73. *reposal* – placing

75. *faithed* – believed
77. *character* – handwriting
78. *suggestion* – instigation
78. *practice* – plot
79. "You must think that everyone in the world is stupid"
81. *pregnant* – obvious
81. *potential* – powerful
83. "O unnatural and hardened villain!"
84. *got* – fathered
Stage Direction: *Tucket* – a trumpet fanfare

91. *capable* – able to inherit

Enter Cornwall, Regan, and Attendants.

97. *father's godson* – Regan has begun her campaign to discredit Lear. She is suggesting that Edgar's plot can be traced to Lear's influence on him.

103. *consort* – company

106. *expense* – spending

113. *childlike* – appropriate to a son
115. *bewray* – inform me of

120. *purpose* – plans
121. *strength* – authority; name

130. *threading* – travelling through the
131. *prize* – importance

134. *differences* – quarrels

CORNWALL: How now, my noble friend? Since I came hither
   (Which I can call but now) I have heard strange news.
REGAN: If it be true, all vengeance comes too short
   Which can pursue the offender. How dost, my Lord?
GLOUCESTER: O Madam, my old heart is cracked, it's cracked!
REGAN: What, did my father's godson seek your life?
   He whom my father named, your Edgar?
GLOUCESTER: O Lady, Lady, shame would have it hid.
REGAN: Was he not companion with the riotous knights   100
   That tend upon my father?
GLOUCESTER: I know not, madam. 'Tis too bad, too bad!
EDMUND: Yes, Madam, he was of that consort.
REGAN: No marvel then though he were ill affected.
   'Tis they have put him on the old man's death,
   To have the expense and waste of his revenues.
   I have this present evening from my sister
   Been well informed of them, and with such cautions
   That, if they come to sojourn at my house,
   I'll not be there.   110
CORNWALL: Nor I, assure thee, Regan.
   Edmund, I hear that you have shown your father
   A childlike office.
EDMUND: It was my duty, Sir.
GLOUCESTER: He did bewray his practice, and received
   This hurt you see, striving to apprehend him.
CORNWALL: Is he pursued?
GLOUCESTER: Ay, my good lord.
CORNWALL: If he be taken, he shall never more
   Be feared of doing harm. Make your own purpose,   120
   How in my strength you please. For you, Edmund,
   Whose virtue and obedience doth this instant
   So much commend itself, you shall be ours.
   Natures of such deep trust we shall much need.
   You we first seize on.
EDMUND: I shall serve you, Sir,
   Truly, however else.
GLOUCESTER: For him I thank your Grace.
CORNWALL: You know not why we came to visit you, —
REGAN: Thus out of season, threading dark-eyed night   130
   Occasions, noble Gloucester, of some prize,
   Wherein we must have use of your advice.
   Our father he hath writ, so hath our sister,
   Of differences, which I best thought it fit

To answer from our home. The several messengers
From hence attend dispatch. Our good old friend,
Lay comforts to your bosom, and bestow
Your needful counsel to our businesses,
Which craves the instant use.

GLOUCESTER: I serve you, Madam.   140
Your Graces are right welcome.

Exeunt. Flourish.

136. *attend dispatch* – are waiting to be sent
139. *craves* – requires
139. *instant* – immediate

Act Two
Scene 2

Before Gloucester's castle.

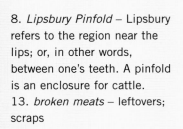

Oswald comes upon Kent, who berates and beats him until they are interrupted by the arrival of Cornwall and Regan. As punishment, Kent is put in the stocks even though he carries messages from the King. Kent reads in a letter that Cordelia is returning from France to assist her father.

8. *Lipsbury Pinfold* – Lipsbury refers to the region near the lips; or, in other words, between one's teeth. A pinfold is an enclosure for cattle.

13. *broken meats* – leftovers; scraps

14 – 15. *three-suited ... knave* – A series of insults suggesting that Oswald is nothing more than a menial servant pretending to be a gentleman. Servants were traditionally given three suits; a hundred pounds was the least amount of money a gentleman would have; and a gentleman would wear silk stockings, not woollen (worsted) ones.

17. *One-trunk-inheriting* – Oswald's possessions would fit in one trunk.

18. *bawd* – pimp

19. *composition* – combination

22. *addition* – titles (names that Kent has called him)

25. *varlet* – rogue; base servant

Enter Kent and Oswald, severally.

OSWALD: Good dawning to thee, friend. Art of this house?
KENT: Ay.
OSWALD: Where may we set our horses?
KENT: In the mire.
OSWALD: Prithee, if thou lov'st me, tell me.
KENT: I love thee not.
OSWALD: Why then, I care not for thee.
KENT: If I had thee in Lipsbury Pinfold, I would make thee care for me.
OSWALD: Why dost thou use me thus? I know thee not.   10
KENT: Fellow, I know thee.
OSWALD: What dost thou know me for?
KENT: A knave, a rascal, an eater of broken meats. A base, proud, shallow, beggarly, three-suited, hundred-pound, filthy, worsted-stocking knave. A lily-livered, action-taking, whoreson, glass-gazing, superserviceable, finical rogue. One-trunk-inheriting slave. One that wouldst be a bawd in way of good service, and art nothing but the composition of a knave, beggar, coward, pander, and the son and heir of a mongrel bitch. One whom I will beat   20
into clamorous whining, if thou deniest the least syllable of thy addition.
OSWALD: Why, what a monstrous fellow art thou, thus to rail on one that is neither known of thee nor knows thee!
KENT: What a brazen-faced varlet art thou, to deny thou knowest me! Is it two days ago since I beat thee and tripped up thy heels before the King?

[Draws his sword.]

Draw, you rogue! For, though it be night, yet the moon shines. I'll make a sop of the moonshine of you. Draw, you whoreson cullionly barbermonger! Draw!   30

OSWALD: Away! I have nothing to do with thee.

KENT: Draw, you rascal! You come with letters against the King, and take Vanity the puppet's part against the royalty of her father. Draw, you rogue, or I'll so carbonado your shanks! Draw, you rascal! Come your ways!

OSWALD: Help, ho! Murder! Help!

KENT: Strike, you slave! Stand, rogue! Stand, you neat slave! Strike!

[Beats him.]

OSWALD: Help, ho! Murder! Murder!

Enter Edmund, with his rapier drawn, Gloucester, Cornwall, Regan, Servants.

EDMUND: How now? What's the matter? Part.   40

KENT: With you, goodman boy, if you please! Come, I'll flesh ye! Come on, young master!

GLOUCESTER: Weapons? Arms? What's the matter here?

CORNWALL: Keep peace, upon your lives! He dies that strikes again. What is the matter?

REGAN: The messengers from our sister and the King.

CORNWALL: What is your difference? Speak.

OSWALD: I am scarce in breath, my Lord.

KENT: No marvel, you have so bestirred your valour. You cowardly rascal, nature disclaims in thee. A tailor made   50 thee.

CORNWALL: Thou art a strange fellow. A tailor make a man?

KENT: Ay, a tailor, sir. A stonecutter or a painter could not have made him so ill, though they had been but two years of the trade.

CORNWALL: Speak yet, how grew your quarrel?

OSWALD: This ancient ruffian, sir, whose life I have spared at suit of his grey beard —

KENT: Thou whoreson zed! Thou unnecessary letter! My Lord, if you will give me leave, I will tread this unbolted villain   60 into mortar and daub the walls of a jakes with him. Spare my grey beard, you wagtail?

29. *make a sop* – fill with holes (that could soak up moonshine)

30. *cullionly barbermonger* – base frequenter of barbershops

33. *Vanity the puppet* – i.e., Goneril. *Vanity* was a common character in the morality plays, which were often performed as puppet shows.

34. *carbonado* – cut into strips

37. *neat* – foolish

42. *flesh ye* – give you your first taste of blood

49. *bestirred* – exercised

50. *disclaims in thee* – denies any part in your creation

59. *zed* – The letter zed or zee was not included in the Latin alphabet and was usually omitted from early dictionaries.

61. *jakes* – bathroom; privy

Act Two • Scene 2

70. *intrince* – intricate; entangled

70. *Smooth* – flatter

73. *Renege* – deny

73. *halcyon* – a kingfisher, whose body could serve as a weathervane, according to Elizabethan beliefs. Kent is accusing Oswald of being variable and fickle with his allegiances.

78. *Sarum Plain* – Salisbury Plain. See map on page 14.

79. *Camelot* – the legendary site of King Arthur's castle

82. *contraries* – opposites

85. "His face does not please me."

92. *doth affect* – pretends; puts on

93 – 94. *constrains ... nature* – distorts or hides his true nature

99. *silly-ducking observants* – bowing attendants

102. *allowance* – approval

104. *Phoebus* – god of the sun

106. *dialect* – usual way of speaking

106. *discommend* – speak critically of

CORNWALL: Peace, sirrah!
    You beastly knave, know you no reverence?
KENT: Yes, sir, but anger hath a privilege.
CORNWALL: Why art thou angry?
KENT: That such a slave as this should wear a sword,
    Who wears no honesty. Such smiling rogues as these,
    Like rats, oft bite the holy cords a-twain
    Which are too intrince to unloose. Smooth every passion   70
    That in the natures of their lords rebel;
    Being oil to fire, snow to their colder moods;
    Renege, affirm, and turn their halcyon beaks
    With every gale and vary of their masters,
    Knowing naught, like dogs, but following.
    A plague upon your epileptic visage!
    Smile you my speeches, as I were a fool?
    Goose, if I had you upon Sarum Plain,
    I'd drive ye cackling home to Camelot.
CORNWALL: What, art thou mad, old fellow?   80
GLOUCESTER: How fell you out? Say that.
KENT: No contraries hold more antipathy
    Than I and such a knave.
CORNWALL: Why dost thou call him knave? What is his fault?
KENT: His countenance likes me not.
CORNWALL: No more perchance does mine, nor his, nor hers.
KENT: Sir, 'tis my occupation to be plain.
    I have seen better faces in my time
    Than stands on any shoulder that I see
    Before me at this instant.   90
CORNWALL: This is some fellow
    Who, having been praised for bluntness, doth affect
    A saucy roughness, and constrains the garb
    Quite from his nature. He cannot flatter, he.
    An honest mind and plain, he must speak truth!
    And they will take it, so; if not, he's plain.
    These kind of knaves I know, which in this plainness
    Harbour more craft and more corrupter ends
    Than twenty silly-ducking observants,
    That stretch their duties nicely.   100
KENT: Sir, in good faith, in sincere verity,
    Under the allowance of your great aspect,
    Whose influence, like the wreath of radiant fire
    On flickering Phoebus' front, —
CORNWALL: What mean'st by this?
KENT: To go out of my dialect, which you discommend so
    much. I know, sir, I am no flatterer. He that beguiled you

in a plain accent was a plain knave, which, for my part,
I will not be, though I should win your displeasure to
entreat me to it.   110
CORNWALL: What was the offence you gave him?
OSWALD: I never gave him any.
　　It pleased the King his master very late
　　To strike at me, upon his misconstruction.
　　When he, compact, and flattering his displeasure,
　　Tripped me behind. Being down, insulted, railed
　　And put upon him such a deal of man,
　　That worthied him, got praises of the King
　　For him attempting who was self-subdued;
　　And, in the fleshment of this dread exploit,   120
　　Drew on me here again.
KENT: None of these rogues and cowards
　　But Ajax is their Fool.
CORNWALL: Fetch forth the stocks!
　　You stubborn ancient knave, you reverend braggart,
　　We'll teach you —
KENT: Sir, I am too old to learn.
　　Call not your stocks for me. I serve the King,
　　On whose employment I was sent to you.
　　You shall do small respect, show too bold malice   130
　　Against the grace and person of my master,
　　Stocking his messenger.
CORNWALL: Fetch forth the stocks!
　　As I have life and honour, there shall he sit till noon.
REGAN: Till noon? Till night, my Lord, and all night too!
KENT: Why, Madam, if I were your father's dog,
　　You should not use me so.
REGAN: Sir, being his knave, I will.
CORNWALL: This is a fellow of the self-same colour
　　Our sister speaks of. Come, bring away the stocks!   140

Stocks brought out.

GLOUCESTER: Let me beseech your Grace not to do so.
　　His fault is much, and the good King his master
　　Will check him for it. Your purposed low correction
　　Is such as basest and contemned'st wretches
　　For pilferings and most common trespasses
　　Are punished with. The King must take it ill
　　That he, so slightly valued in his messenger,
　　Should have him thus restrained.
CORNWALL: I'll answer that.

stocks

114. *misconstruction* – misunderstanding
115. *compact* – in a compact with (the King)
117. "Made himself out to be such a hero"
119. *attempting* – attacking
120. *fleshment* – blood-thirstiness; excitement
122 – 123. In Homer's *Iliad*, the Greek hero Ajax, a rather dim-witted person, was treated as a fool by *rogues and cowards*. Cornwall takes this reference personally, believing that Kent has equated him with Ajax.
124. *stocks* – a form of punishment consisting of a frame with holes for confining the ankles and sometimes the wrists

143. *check* – punish
144. *contemned'st* – most despicable

156. *rubbed* – interfered with
157. *watched* – gone without sleep
159. *fortune ... heels* – luck may change for the worse
161. *ill taken* – badly received
162. *approve ... saw* – confirm the old saying
163. *heaven's benediction* – the comfort of shade
165. *beacon* – sun
167 – 168. *Nothing ... misery* – "When one is in misery, the slightest relief seems a miracle."
170. *obscured* – disguised

168 – 172. No one has satisfactorily explained how Cordelia could have travelled to France, received word from Kent, and sent back a reply announcing her imminent return to England in such a short period of time. Shakespeare frequently compressed time to make the action more dramatic.

175. The Elizabethans believed that people's lives followed a cyclical pattern, as if each person were attached to a part of a large wheel. The constant turning of the wheel explained the rise and fall of a person's fortune.

Fortune's wheel

REGAN: My sister may receive it much more worse,   150
    To have her gentleman abused, assaulted,
    For following her affairs. Put in his legs.

[Kent is put in the stocks.]

Come, my good Lord, away.

[Exeunt all but Gloucester and Kent.]

GLOUCESTER: I am sorry for thee, friend. 'Tis the Duke's
    pleasure,
    Whose disposition, all the world well knows,
    Will not be rubbed nor stopped. I'll entreat for thee.
KENT: Pray do not, sir. I have watched and travelled hard.
    Some time I shall sleep out, the rest I'll whistle.
    A good man's fortune may grow out at heels.
    Give you good morrow.   160
GLOUCESTER: The Duke's to blame in this. 'Twill be ill taken.

Exit.

KENT: Good King, that must approve the common saw,
    Thou out of heaven's benediction com'st
    To the warm sun!
    Approach, thou beacon to this under globe,
    That by thy comfortable beams I may
    Peruse this letter. Nothing almost sees miracles
    But misery. I know 'tis from Cordelia,
    Who hath most fortunately been informed
    Of my obscured course, and shall find time   170
    From this enormous state, seeking to give
    Losses their remedies. All weary and overwatched,
    Take vantage, heavy eyes, not to behold
    This shameful lodging.
    Fortune, good night. Smile once more, turn thy wheel.

Sleeps.

Act Two
Scene 3

A wood in the open country.

Enter Edgar.

EDGAR: I heard myself proclaimed,
And by the happy hollow of a tree
Escaped the hunt. No port is free, no place
That guard and most unusual vigilance
Does not attend my taking. Whiles I may 'scape,
I will preserve myself. And am bethought
To take the basest and most poorest shape
That ever penury, in contempt of man,
Brought near to beast. My face I'll grime with filth,
Blanket my loins, elf all my hair in knots,   10
And with presented nakedness outface
The winds and persecutions of the sky.
The country gives me proof and precedent
Of Bedlam beggars, who, with roaring voices,
Strike in their numbed and mortified bare arms
Pins, wooden pricks, nails, sprigs of rosemary.
And with this horrible object, from low farms,
Poor pelting villages, sheepcotes, and mills,
Sometime with lunatic bans, sometime with prayers,
Enforce their charity. "Poor Turlygod! Poor Tom!"   20
That's something yet! Edgar I nothing am.

Exit.

Edgar has escaped capture by hiding in a hollow of a tree. To remain safe, he disguises himself as a mad beggar.

1. *proclaimed* – declared an outlaw, to be killed on sight
2. *happy* – lucky
6. *am bethought* – have decided
8. *penury* – poverty
10. *elf* – tangle
11. *outface* – defy

14. *Bedlam beggars* – Aggressive beggars who frequently stuck pins in their arms to prove they were mad. Because their mental disturbance was relatively mild, they were not institutionalized. A common name for a Bedlam beggar was *Poor Tom.*

Bedlam beggar

20. *Turlygod* – nonsense
21. "As a madman, I have hope; as Edgar, I am nothing."

British psychiatrist Nigel Bark argues that Edgar provides a "classic description of chronic schizophrenia." He further speculates that Shakespeare had a real model from which to work. This refutes the modern view that schizophrenia made its first appearance late in the 18th century.

Act Two
Scene 4

Before Gloucester's castle.

[Kent in the stocks.]
Enter Lear, Fool, and Gentleman.

LEAR: 'Tis strange that they should so depart from home,
　And not send back my messenger.
GENTLEMAN: As I learned,
　The night before there was no purpose in them
　Of this remove.
KENT: Hail to thee, noble master!
LEAR: Ha!
　Mak'st thou this shame thy pastime?
KENT: No, my lord.

Lear arrives at Gloucester's castle and is angered that Kent has been put into the stocks. His fury increases when he learns that Regan and Cornwall refuse to speak with him. When Goneril arrives, the two sisters join forces and tell Lear that they will not allow him to stay with them unless he dismisses all of his attendants. In a rage, Lear leaves the castle as a violent storm erupts.

2. *my messenger* – Kent

5. *remove* – departure

FOOL: Ha, ha! Look! He wears cruel garters. Horses are tied   10
by the heads, dogs and bears by the neck, monkeys by
the loins, and men by the legs. When a man's over-lusty
at legs, then he wears wooden nether-stocks.
LEAR: What's he that hath so much thy place mistook
To set thee here?
KENT: It is both he and she,
Your son and daughter.
LEAR: No.
KENT: Yes.
LEAR: No, I say.   20
KENT: I say, yea.
LEAR: No, no, they would not.
KENT: Yes, they have.
LEAR: By Jupiter, I swear, no!
KENT: By Juno, I swear, ay!
LEAR: They durst not do it.
They could not, would not do it. 'Tis worse than murder,
To do upon respect such violent outrage.
Resolve me with all modest haste which way
Thou might'st deserve or they impose this usage,   30
Coming from us.
KENT: My lord, when at their home
I did commend your Highness' letters to them,
Ere I was risen from the place that showed
My duty kneeling, came there a reeking post,

12. *over-lusty* – too active or restless (in other words, a vagabond)

13. *nether-stocks* – stockings

25. *Juno* – queen of the gods and wife to Jupiter

28. *respect* – the respect due to the King's messenger

35. *post* – messenger (Oswald)

38. *spite of intermission* – not caring that he had interrupted the mission

40. *meiny* – servants; followers

52. *wear rags* – give away their property

53. *blind* – insensitive; indifferent

54. *bear bags* – keep their moneybags

58. *dolours* – sorrows; also a pun on *dollars*

59. *tell* – count; relate

60 – 61. Lear feels a choking, smothering sensation rising up from below his heart. This symptom of sudden fear or panic was called *mother* or *hysterica passio* (affliction of the womb) because of the false belief that women suffered it more often than men.

62. *element's* – proper place is

69. *And* – If

72 – 77. The Fool refers to Aesop's fable of the self-reliant ant who stores food for the winter. In so doing, the Fool suggests that most of Lear's followers have left him because they know there is no value in working for an old, powerless King (*labouring in the winter*). *Stinking* may be a reference to the smell of misfortune. Lear can be likened to a *great wheel* rolling uncontrollably downhill, crushing everyone who is hanging on.

Stewed in his haste, half breathless, panting forth
From Goneril his mistress salutations.
Delivered letters, spite of intermission,
Which presently they read; on whose contents,
They summoned up their meiny, straight took horse,   40
Commanded me to follow and attend
The leisure of their answer, gave me cold looks,
And meeting here the other messenger,
Whose welcome I perceived had poisoned mine —
Being the very fellow which of late
Displayed so saucily against your Highness —
Having more man than wit about me, drew.
He raised the house with loud and coward cries.
Your son and daughter found this trespass worth
The shame which here it suffers.   50

FOOL: Winter's not gone yet, if the wild geese fly that way.

> Fathers that wear rags
>   Do make their children blind,
> But fathers that bear bags
>   Shall see their children kind.
> Fortune, that arrant whore,
>   Never turns the key to the poor.

But for all this, thou shalt have as many dolours for thy daughters as thou canst tell in a year.

LEAR: O, how this mother swells up toward my heart!   60
Hysterica passio! Down, thou climbing sorrow!
Thy element's below! Where is this daughter?

KENT: With the Earl, Sir, here within.

LEAR: Follow me not. Stay here.

Exit.

GENTLEMAN: Made you no more offence but what you
    speak of?

KENT: None.
How chance the King comes with so small a number?

FOOL: And thou hadst been set in the stocks for that question,
    thou'dst well deserved it.   70

KENT: Why, Fool?

FOOL: We'll set thee to school to an ant, to teach thee there's
    no labouring in the winter. All that follow their noses are
    led by their eyes but blind men, and there's not a nose
    among twenty but can smell him that's stinking. Let go

thy hold when a great wheel runs down a hill, lest it
break thy neck with following it. But the great one that
goes upward, let him draw thee after. When a wise man
gives thee better counsel, give me mine again. I would
have none but knaves follow it, since a fool gives it.   80

> That sir which serves and seeks for gain,
>   And follows but for form,
> Will pack when it begins to rain
>   And leave thee in the storm.
> But I will tarry; the fool will stay,
>   And let the wise man fly.
> The knave turns Fool that runs away;
>   The Fool no knave, perdy.

KENT: Where learned you this, Fool?
FOOL: Not in the stocks, Fool.   90

Enter Lear and Gloucester.

LEAR: Deny to speak with me? They are sick? They are weary?
    They have travelled all the night? Mere fetches, ay,
    The images of revolt and flying off!
    Fetch me a better answer.
GLOUCESTER: My dear Lord,
    You know the fiery quality of the Duke,
    How unremovable and fixed he is
    In his own course.
LEAR: Vengeance! Plague! Death! Confusion!
    Fiery? What quality? Why, Gloucester, Gloucester,   100
    I'd speak with the Duke of Cornwall and his wife.
GLOUCESTER: Well, my good Lord, I have informed them so.
LEAR: Informed them? Dost thou understand me, man?
GLOUCESTER: Ay, my good Lord.
LEAR: The King would speak with Cornwall. The dear father
    Would with his daughter speak, commands, tends service.
    Are they informed of this? My breath and blood!
    Fiery? The fiery Duke? Tell the hot Duke that —
    No, but not yet! May be he is not well.
    Infirmity doth still neglect all office   110
    Whereto our health is bound. We are not ourselves
    When nature, being oppressed, commands the mind
    To suffer with the body. I'll forbear;
    And am fallen out with my more headier will,
    To take the indisposed and sickly fit
    For the sound man. Death on my state!

82. *form* – public show

85. *tarry* – stay

88. *perdy* – par Dieu (French for "by God")

92. *fetches* – lies; tricks

97. *unremovable* – stubborn

110. *office* – duty

113. *forbear* – be patient
114. *more headier will* – impulsiveness
116. *Death ... state!* – "An insult to my royal state!"

Act Two • Scene 4

118. *remotion* – aloofness; disregard
119. *practice* – a trick or scheme
119. *Give me* – release

126. *cockney* – perhaps an inexperienced or foolish person who is unaware that eels need to be killed before they are placed in the pie shell *(paste)*. This person rapped *(knapped)* the eels, just as Lear thumps on his own chest.
130. *buttered his hay* – Dishonest persons would profit by greasing the hay they sold, knowing that horses would not eat it.

136 – 137. "I would refuse to be buried with your mother because her tomb would contain an adulteress." The implication is that Regan would not be Lear's daughter if she were not glad to see him.

139. *naught* – wicked

[Looking at Kent.]

　　　　　　　　　　　　　　　　Wherefore
Should he sit here? This act persuades me
That this remotion of the Duke and her
Is practice only. Give me my servant forth.
Go tell the Duke and his wife I'd speak with them,　　120
Now, presently. Bid them come forth and hear me,
Or at their chamber door I'll beat the drum
Till it cry sleep to death.
GLOUCESTER: I would have all well betwixt you.

Exit.

LEAR: O me, my heart, my rising heart! But down!
FOOL: Cry to it, Nuncle, as the cockney did to the eels when
　　　she put them in the paste alive. She knapped them on the
　　　coxcombs with a stick, and cried "Down, wantons,
　　　down!" 'Twas her brother that, in pure kindness to his
　　　horse, buttered his hay.　　130

Enter Cornwall, Regan, Gloucester, Servants.

LEAR: Good morrow to you both.
CORNWALL: Hail to your Grace!

Kent here set at liberty.

REGAN: I am glad to see your Highness.
LEAR: Regan, I think you are. I know what reason
　　　I have to think so. If thou shouldst not be glad,
　　　I would divorce me from thy mother's tomb,
　　　Sepulchring an adultress.

[To Kent.]

　　　　　　　　　　　　　　O, are you free?
Some other time for that.

[Exit Kent.]

　　　　　　　　　　　　　　Beloved Regan,
Thy sister's naught. O Regan, she hath tied
Sharp-toothed unkindness, like a vulture, here!　　140

[Points to his heart.]

I can scarce speak to thee. Thou'lt not believe
With how depraved a quality — O Regan!

REGAN: I pray you, sir, take patience. I have hope
You less know how to value her desert
Than she to scant her duty.

LEAR: Say, how is that?

REGAN: I cannot think my sister in the least
Would fail her obligation. If, Sir, perchance
She have restrained the riots of your followers,
'Tis on such ground, and to such wholesome end,   150
As clears her from all blame.

LEAR: My curses on her!

REGAN: O, Sir, you are old!
Nature in you stands on the very verge
Of her confine. You should be ruled, and led
By some discretion that discerns your state
Better than you yourself. Therefore I pray you
That to our sister you do make return.
Say you have wronged her.

LEAR: Ask her forgiveness?   160
Do you but mark how this becomes the house:
"Dear daughter, I confess that I am old. *[Kneels.]*
Age is unnecessary. On my knees I beg
That you'll vouchsafe me raiment, bed, and food."

REGAN: Good sir, no more! These are unsightly tricks.
Return you to my sister.

LEAR: *[Rises.]* Never, Regan!
She hath abated me of half my train.
Looked black upon me, struck me with her tongue,
Most serpent-like, upon the very heart.   170
All the stored vengeances of Heaven fall
On her ingrateful top! Strike her young bones,
You taking airs, with lameness!

CORNWALL: Fie, Sir, fie!

LEAR: You nimble lightnings, dart your blinding flames
Into her scornful eyes! Infect her beauty,
You fen-sucked fogs, drawn by the powerful sun,
To fall and blast her pride!

REGAN: O the blest gods! So will you wish on me
When the rash mood is on.   180

LEAR: No, Regan, thou shalt never have my curse.
Thy tender-hefted nature shall not give
Thee over to harshness. Her eyes are fierce, but thine

144. *desert* – merit; deserving
145. *scant* – neglect

"The 'serpent's tooth' is not really the thankless child. Goneril and Regan thank their father profusely and then betray him. The serpent's tooth that cuts Lear is his desire to be thanked, to be flattered, to be loved by his daughters."
– Isabelle Emery (b. 1954), Canadian scholar

155. *confine* – limit (in terms of years of life)

161. *house* – family relations. Lear is being sarcastic; he does not think that a father should kneel for forgiveness from his daughter.

164. *vouchsafe* – grant
164. *raiment* – clothing
168. *abated* – deprived

172. *top* – head
173. *taking* – blasting

177. *fen-sucked* – rising from swamps or marshes

182. *hefted* – hearted

186. *scant my sizes* – reduce my allowances
187. *oppose the bolt* – lock the door

196. *approves* – confirms

198. *easy-borrowed* – acquired without justification

205. *sway* – power

212. *dotage* – foolish actions of old persons
213. *sides* – breast (which he expects to burst because of his pain)
216. *advancement* – treatment; reward

Do comfort, and not burn. 'Tis not in thee
To grudge my pleasures, to cut off my train,
To bandy hasty words, to scant my sizes,
And, in conclusion, to oppose the bolt
Against my coming in. Thou better know'st
The offices of nature, bond of childhood,
Effects of courtesy, dues of gratitude.   190
Thy half of the kingdom hast thou not forgot,
Wherein I thee endowed.

REGAN: Good sir, to the purpose.

LEAR: Who put my man in the stocks?

Tucket within.

CORNWALL: What trumpet's that?

REGAN: I know it, my sister's. This approves her letter,
That she would soon be here.

Enter Oswald.

                          Is your lady come?

LEAR: This is a slave, whose easy-borrowed pride
Dwells in the fickle grace of her he follows.
Out, varlet, from my sight!   200

CORNWALL: What means your Grace?

Enter Goneril.

LEAR: Who stocked my servant? Regan, I have good hope
Thou didst not know on it.
Who comes here? O heavens!
If you do love old men, if your sweet sway
Allow obedience, if yourselves are old,
Make it your cause! Send down, and take my part!
[To Goneril.] Art not ashamed to look upon this beard?
O Regan! Wilt thou take her by the hand?

GONERIL: Why not by the hand, sir? How have I offended? 210
All's not offence that indiscretion finds
And dotage terms so.

LEAR: O sides, you are too tough!
Will you yet hold? How came my man in the stocks?

CORNWALL: I set him there, Sir. But his own disorders
Deserved much less advancement.

LEAR: You! Did you?

66

REGAN: I pray you, father, being weak, seem so.
    If, till the expiration of your month,
    You will return and sojourn with my sister,   220
    Dismissing half your train, come then to me.
    I am now from home, and out of that provision
    Which shall be needful for your entertainment.
LEAR: Return to her, and fifty men dismissed?
    No, rather I abjure all roofs, and choose   *225. abjure* – renounce
    To wage against the enmity of the air,
    To be a comrade with the wolf and owl,
    Necessity's sharp pinch! Return with her!
    Why, the hot-blooded France, that dowerless took   *229. hot-blooded* – passionate
    Our youngest born, I could as well be brought   230
    To knee his throne, and, squire-like, pension beg
    To keep base life afoot. Return with her!
    Persuade me rather to be slave and sumpter   *233. sumpter* – packhorse
    To this detested groom.

[Points at Oswald.]

GONERIL: At your choice, Sir.
LEAR: I prithee, daughter, do not make me mad.
    I will not trouble thee, my child. Farewell.
    We'll no more meet, no more see one another.
    But yet thou art my flesh, my blood, my daughter.
    Or rather a disease that's in my flesh,   240
    Which I must needs call mine. Thou art a boil,
    A plague sore, an embossed carbuncle,   *242. embossed carbuncle* –
    In my corrupted blood. But I'll not chide thee.   swollen boil
    Let shame come when it will, I do not call it.
    I do not bid the Thunder-bearer shoot   *245. Thunder-bearer* – the god
    Nor tell tales of thee to high-judging Jove.   Jupiter or Jove
    Mend when thou canst; be better at thy leisure.
    I can be patient. I can stay with Regan,
    I and my hundred knights.
REGAN: Not altogether so.   250
    I looked not for you yet, nor am provided
    For your fit welcome. Give ear, Sir, to my sister,
    For those that mingle reason with your passion
    Must be content to think you old, and so —
    But she knows what she does.
LEAR: Is this well spoken?
REGAN: I dare avouch it, sir. What, fifty followers?   *257. avouch* – affirm
    Is it not well? What should you need of more?

259. *sith ... charge* – since ... expense

265. *slack ye* – neglect you

272. *depositaries* – trustees
273. *reservation* – legal stipulation

277. *well-favoured* – pleasing; attractive

288 – 289. *Our ... superfluous* – "Even the poorest beggars have some possessions that are not absolutely necessary."

Yea, or so many, sith that both charge and danger
Speak 'gainst so great a number? How in one house   260
Should many people, under two commands,
Hold amity? 'Tis hard; almost impossible.
GONERIL: Why might not you, my lord, receive attendance
From those that she calls servants, or from mine?
REGAN: Why not, my lord? If then they chanced to slack ye,
We could control them. If you will come to me
(For now I spy a danger), I entreat you
To bring but five-and-twenty. To no more
Will I give place or notice.
LEAR: I gave you all —   270
REGAN: And in good time you gave it!
LEAR: Made you my guardians, my depositaries,
But kept a reservation to be followed
With such a number. What, must I come to you
With five-and-twenty? Regan, said you so?
REGAN: And speak it again my Lord. No more with me.
LEAR: Those wicked creatures yet do look well-favoured
When others are more wicked. Not being the worst
Stands in some rank of praise.

[To Goneril.]

I'll go with thee.   280
Thy fifty yet doth double five-and-twenty,
And thou art twice her love.
GONERIL: Hear, me, my lord.
What need you five-and-twenty, ten, or five,
To follow in a house where twice so many
Have a command to tend you?
REGAN: What need one?
LEAR: O, reason not the need! Our basest beggars
Are in the poorest thing superfluous.
Allow not nature more than nature needs,   290
Man's life is cheap as beast's. Thou art a lady.
If only to go warm were gorgeous,
Why, nature needs not what thou gorgeous wear'st
Which scarcely keeps thee warm. But, for true need —
You heavens, give me that patience, patience I need!
You see me here, you gods, a poor old man,
As full of grief as age, wretched in both.
If it be you that stirs these daughters' hearts
Against their father, fool me not so much
To bear it tamely. Touch me with noble anger,   300
And let not women's weapons, water drops,

Stain my man's cheeks! — No, you unnatural hags!
I will have such revenges on you both
That all the world shall — I will do such things,
What they are yet, I know not, but they shall be
The terrors of the earth! You think I'll weep.
No, I'll not weep. I have full cause of weeping,

Storm and tempest.

But this heart shall break into a hundred thousand flaws   308. *flaws* – fragments
Or ere I'll weep. O Fool, I shall go mad!

Exeunt Lear, Gloucester, Kent, and Fool.

CORNWALL: Let us withdraw. 'Twill be a storm.   310
REGAN: This house is little. The old man and his people
    Cannot be well bestowed.
GONERIL: 'Tis his own blame, hath put himself from rest   314. "And he should suffer the consequences of his foolishness."
315. *his particular* – him personally
    And must needs taste his folly.
REGAN: For his particular, I'll receive him gladly,
    But not one follower.
GONERIL: So am I purposed.
    Where is my Lord of Gloucester?

Enter Gloucester.

CORNWALL: Followed the old man forth. He is returned.
GLOUCESTER: The King is in high rage.   320
CORNWALL: Whither is he going?
GLOUCESTER: He calls to horse, but will I know not whither.   322. *whither* – where
323. *leads himself* – insists on having his way
CORNWALL: 'Tis best to give him way. He leads himself.
GONERIL: My lord, entreat him by no means to stay.
GLOUCESTER: Alack, the night comes on, and the bleak winds
    Do sorely ruffle. For many miles about
    There's scarce a bush.
REGAN: O, sir, to wilful men,
    The injuries that they themselves procure
    Must be their schoolmasters. Shut up your doors.   330
    He is attended with a desperate train,   331. *desperate train* – Because Lear's knights are armed and desperate, they are dangerous. Perhaps Regan says this to justify locking the doors.
    And what they may incense him to, being apt
    To have his ear abused, wisdom bids fear.
CORNWALL: Shut up your doors, my lord. 'Tis a wild night.
    My Regan counsels well. Come out of the storm.

Exeunt.

❧ ❧ ❧

Act Two Considerations

ACT TWO Scene 1

▶ In line 18, Edmund calls upon the goddess Fortune. The symbol of Fortune's wheel recurs throughout this play. (See note for line 175 on page 58.) Draw a diagram of a large wheel, with the top of the wheel representing the best possible fortune. Where would you place Edmund on this wheel at the beginning of Act One? By the end of Act Two, Scene 1, where would you place Edmund?

As you read the play, watch for references to Fortune's wheel. When a reference occurs, mark Edmund's position on your diagram. Also record line references and brief summaries of events that mark Edmund's rise and fall in fortune.

Repeat this process for Edgar.

ACT TWO Scene 2

▶ Imagine that you witnessed the altercation between Kent and Oswald and the police have asked you to write a statement of what you saw. Assume that you do not know either of the men involved. Write the statement, expressing an opinion about who is more responsible for the disturbance.

▶ How does Kent conduct himself during his interrogation by Cornwall and Regan? If you were his friend, what advice would you give him?

ACT TWO Scene 3

▶ If you were adapting this play to give it a modern-day setting, what disguise would you choose for Edgar? Explain your reasoning.

▶ Kent takes pride in being honest and speaking plainly. How honestly has he described the events that lead to his confinement in the stocks?

▶ Shakespeare included few stage directions in his plays, so it is impossible to know what he intended for any speech or scene. Each new director of Shakespeare's plays must therefore establish her or his interpretation. Imagine you are directing *King Lear*. How would you present Scene 4 from the time of Goneril's arrival to the end? Write a series of stage directions that describe the gestures and actions each actor should perform and what tone of voice each should use. Create enough directions to show how the scene develops and the characters behave.

▶ Some critics have suggested that the arrival of the storm is contrived and unrealistic. What dramatic purposes do you think the storm might serve? Write a paragraph in which you defend or criticize Shakespeare's introduction of the storm at the end of this scene.

Act Three
Scene 1

A heath.

Storm still. Enter Kent and a Gentleman, severally.

KENT: Who's there, besides foul weather?
GENTLEMAN: One minded like the weather, most unquietly.
KENT: I know you. Where's the King?
GENTLEMAN: Contending with the fretful elements.
    Bids the wind blow the earth into the sea,
    Or swell the curled waters 'bove the main,
    That things might change or cease. Tears his white hair,
    Which the impetuous blasts, with eyeless rage,
    Catch in their fury and make nothing of.
    Strives in his little world of man to outstorm   10
    The to-and-fro-conflicting wind and rain.
    This night, wherein the cub-drawn bear would couch,
    The lion and the belly-pinched wolf
    Keep their fur dry, unbonneted he runs,
    And bids what will take all.
KENT: But who is with him?
GENTLEMAN: None but the Fool, who labours to outjest
    His heart-struck injuries.
KENT: Sir, I do know you,
    And dare upon the warrant of my note   20
    Commend a dear thing to you. There is division
    (Although as yet the face of it be covered
    With mutual cunning) 'twixt Albany and Cornwall,
    Who have — as who have not, that their great stars
    Throned and set high — servants, who seem no less,
    Which are to France the spies and speculations
    Intelligent of our state. What hath been seen,
    Either in snuffs and packings of the Dukes,
    Or the hard rein which both of them have borne

2. *minded* – troubled
6. *main* – mainland
7. *things* – state of affairs; everything
8. *eyeless* – blind
9. *make ... of* – treat with no regard
10. *little world* – microcosm. The human body was considered to be a microcosm or a little world that mirrored the macrocosm or universe.
12. *cub-drawn* – suckled by cubs
12. *couch* – find shelter
13. *belly-pinched* – starving
15. *all* – all the world

17 – 18. "Only the Fool, whose jokes are meant to relieve the King's heart-felt pain."

20. *warrant ... note* – assurance that I know you
21. *Commend* – entrust
21. *division* – a quarrel
24 – 27. Spies among Cornwall's and Albany's servants have told France about the quarrel between the two dukes.
28. *snuffs and packings* – quarrels and plots

31. *furnishings* – pretexts; excuses
33. *scattered* – divided
34. *feet* – footholds

37. *credit* – trustworthiness
38. *Dover* – a strategic port on the southeast coast of England. See map on page 14.
39. *making* – for making a
41. *plain* – complain

48. *out-wall* – outward appearance

55. *to effect* – in their importance
56. *pain* – care; task

Against the old kind King, or something deeper,   30
Whereof, perchance, these are but furnishings —
But, true it is, from France there comes a power
Into this scattered kingdom, who already,
Wise in our negligence, have secret feet
In some of our best ports, and are at point
To show their open banner. Now to you:
If on my credit you dare build so far
To make your speed to Dover, you shall find
Some that will thank you, making just report
Of how unnatural and bemadding sorrow   40
The King hath cause to plain.
I am a gentleman of blood and breeding,
And from some knowledge and assurance offer
This office to you.

GENTLEMAN: I will talk further with you.

KENT: No, do not.
For confirmation that I am much more
Than my out-wall, open this purse and take
What it contains. If you shall see Cordelia,
(As fear not but you shall), show her this ring,   50
And she will tell you who your fellow is
That yet you do not know. Fie on this storm!
I will go seek the King.

GENTLEMAN: Give me your hand. Have you no more to say?

KENT: Few words, but, to effect, more than all yet:
That, when we have found the King (in which your pain
That way, I'll this), he that first lights on him
Holla the other.

Exeunt [severally].

Act Three
Scene 2

Kent finds Lear and the Fool braving the storm. He convinces them to seek shelter in a dry hovel.

Another part of the heath.

Storm still. Enter Lear and Fool.

LEAR: Blow, winds, and crack your cheeks! Rage! Blow!
You cataracts and hurricanoes, spout
Till you have drenched our steeples, drowned the cocks!
You sulph'rous and thought-executing fires,
Vaunt-couriers to oak-cleaving thunderbolts,
Singe my white head! And thou, all-shaking thunder,
Strike flat the thick rotundity of the world,
Crack Nature's moulds, all germens spill at once,
That makes ingrateful man!

FOOL: O Nuncle, court holy-water in a dry house is better　　10
than this rain-water out of door. Good Nuncle, in, and
ask thy daughters' blessing! Here's a night pities neither
wise men nor Fools.

LEAR: Rumble thy bellyful! Spit, fire! Spout, rain!
Nor rain, wind, thunder, fire, are my daughters.
I tax you not, you elements, with unkindness.
I never gave you kingdom, called you children,
You owe me no subscription. Then let fall
Your horrible pleasure. Here I stand your slave,
A poor, infirm, weak, and despised old man.　　20
But yet I call you servile ministers,
That will with two pernicious daughters join
Your high-engendered battles 'gainst a head
So old and white as this! O, ho! 'Tis foul!

FOOL: He that has a house to put his head in has a good
head-piece.

2. *cataracts* – heaven's floodgates
3. *cocks* – weathervanes
4. *thought-executing* – as quick as thought
5. *Vaunt-couriers* – heralds
8. *germens* – seeds. Lear would like to see the world end forever, first by water, then by fire.
10. *court holy-water* – flattering speeches

"*Lear* combines length with rapidity—like the hurricane and the whirlpool, absorbing while it advances. It begins as a stormy day in summer, with brightness; but that brightness is lurid, and anticipates the tempest."
– Samuel Taylor Coleridge (1772–1834), English Romantic poet and critic

16. *tax* – charge; accuse
18. *subscription* – obedience; submission
23. *high-engendered battles* – heavenly armies

27. *codpiece* – a pouch at the crotch of tight-fitting trousers worn by men in the 15th and 16th centuries

27. *house* – find shelter

28. "Before he has a house to live in"

29. *louse* – become infested with lice

31 – 34. "The man who values something worthless and ignores something precious shall suffer for his actions."

35 – 36. *made ... glass* – practised faces in front of a mirror

40. *grace* – his grace, the King. The Fool is the codpiece.

"Lear is joined by the Fool and Kent, Kent being also a fool, as the Fool himself informs him, for we are now in a world where it is folly to be genuinely loyal."
– Northrop Frye (1912 – 1991), Canadian scholar and critic

44. "Terrify even the wild beasts"

51. *pudder* – turmoil

55. *simular* – counterfeit

56. *Caitiff* – wretch

59. *Rive* – split apart

67. *demanding after* – enquiring about

The codpiece that will house
    Before the head has any,
The head and he shall louse,
    So beggars marry many.   30
The man that makes his toe
    What he his heart should make,
Shall of a corn cry woe,
    And turn his sleep to wake.

For there was never yet fair woman but she made mouths in a glass.

Enter Kent.

LEAR: No, I will be the pattern of all patience;
    I will say nothing.
KENT: Who's there?
FOOL: Marry, here's grace and a codpiece. That's a wise man   40
    and a Fool.
KENT: Alas, Sir, are you here? Things that love night
    Love not such nights as these. The wrathful skies
    Gallow the very wanderers of the dark
    And make them keep their caves. Since I was man,
    Such sheets of fire, such bursts of horrid thunder,
    Such groans of roaring wind and rain, I never
    Remember to have heard. Man's nature cannot carry
    The affliction nor the fear.
LEAR: Let the great gods,   50
    That keep this dreadful pudder over our heads,
    Find out their enemies now. Tremble, thou wretch,
    That hast within thee undivulged crimes
    Unwhipped of Justice. Hide thee, thou bloody hand.
    Thou perjured, and thou simular man of virtue
    That art incestuous. Caitiff, in pieces shake
    That under covert and convenient seeming
    Has practised on man's life. Close pent-up guilts,
    Rive your concealing continents, and cry
    These dreadful summoners grace. I am a man   60
    More sinned against than sinning.
KENT: Alack, bareheaded!
    Gracious my lord, hard by here is a hovel.
    Some friendship will it lend you 'gainst the tempest.
    Repose you there, whilst I to this hard house
    (More harder than the stones whereof 'tis raised,
    Which even but now, demanding after you,

Denied me to come in) return, and force
Their scanted courtesy.

LEAR: My wits begin to turn.   70
Come on, my boy. How dost, my boy? Art cold?
I am cold myself. Where is this straw, my fellow?
The art of our necessities is strange,
And can make vile things precious. Come, your hovel.
Poor Fool and knave, I have one part in my heart
That's sorry yet for thee.

FOOL: *[Sings.] He that has and a little tiny wit,*
            With hey, ho, the wind and the rain,
      Must make content with his fortunes fit,
            For the rain it raineth every day.   80

LEAR: True, my good boy. Come, bring us to this hovel.

Exeunt [Lear and Kent].

FOOL: This is a brave night to cool a courtesan.
I'll speak a prophecy ere I go:
When priests are more in word than matter;
When brewers mar their malt with water;
When nobles are their tailors' tutors;
No heretics burned, but wenches' suitors;
When every case in law is right;
No squire in debt nor no poor knight;
When slanders do not live in tongues;   90
Nor cut-purses come not to throngs;
When usurers tell their gold in the field,
And bawds and whores do churches build;
Then shall the realm of Albion
Come to great confusion.
Then comes the time, who lives to see it,
That going shall be used with feet.
This prophecy Merlin shall make, for I live before his
time.

Exit.

69. *scanted* – withheld

73. *art* – alchemy. The Elizabethans were fascinated by alchemy, a chemical philosophy devoted to the discovery of magical practices that could transform lead into gold (*make vile things precious*).

Lear

Only mad fools and English kings go out in the mid night storm.

– Ruth E. Bell, American scholar

82. *courtesan* – prostitute

91. "When pickpockets avoid crowded places"
92. *usurers tell* – money-lenders count
94. *Albion* – England
98. *Merlin* – King Arthur's magician who, according to legend, lived thirteen hundred years after the rule of King Lear.

Merlin

Act Three
Scene 3

Gloucester's castle.

Enter Gloucester and Edmund, with lights.

GLOUCESTER: Alack, alack, Edmund, I like not this unnatural dealing! When I desired their leave that I might pity him, they took from me the use of mine own house, charged me on pain of perpetual displeasure neither to speak of him, entreat for him, or any way sustain him.

EDMUND: Most savage and unnatural!

GLOUCESTER: Go to. Say you nothing. There is division betwixt the Dukes, and a worse matter than that. I have received a letter this night — 'tis dangerous to be spoken. I have locked the letter in my closet. These injuries the King   10
now bears will be revenged home. There is part of a power already footed. We must incline to the King. I will seek him and privily relieve him. Go you and maintain talk with the Duke, that my charity be not of him perceived. If he ask for me, I am ill and gone to bed. Though I die for it, as no less is threatened me, the King my old master must be relieved. There is some strange thing toward, Edmund. Pray you be careful.

Exit.

EDMUND: This courtesy, forbid thee, shall the Duke
Instantly know, and of that letter too.   20
This seems a fair deserving, and must draw me
That which my father loses — no less than all.
The younger rises when the old doth fall.

Exit.

Marginal notes:

Gloucester tells Edmund that he will help Lear, disobeying Cornwall's orders. Gloucester then reveals the location of a letter containing information about the impending French invasion. When Gloucester leaves, Edmund announces that he will betray his father, thereby gaining his father's title.

2. *leave* – permission

11. *home* – fully
12. *footed ... incline to* – landed ... take the side of
13. *privily* – secretly

21. *fair deserving* – deed that will be well rewarded

Act Three
Scene 4

With the storm still raging, Kent, Lear, and the Fool seek shelter in a hovel. There they meet Edgar, who is disguised as a mad beggar. Gloucester arrives and takes them to warmer quarters in the farmhouse of his castle.

The heath. Before a hovel.

Storm still. Enter Lear, Kent, and Fool.

KENT: Here is the place, my lord. Good my Lord, enter.
　　　The tyranny of the open night is too rough
　　　For nature to endure.
LEAR: Let me alone.
KENT: Good my Lord, enter here.
LEAR: Wilt break my heart?
KENT: I had rather break mine own. Good my Lord, enter.
LEAR: Thou think'st 'tis much that this contentious storm
　　　Invades us to the skin. So 'tis to thee.
　　　But where the greater malady is fixed,　　　　　　　10
　　　The lesser is scarce felt. Thou wouldst shun a bear,
　　　But if thy flight lay toward the raging sea,
　　　Thou wouldst meet the bear in the mouth. When the
　　　　　mind's free,
　　　The body's delicate. This tempest in my mind
　　　Doth from my senses take all feeling else
　　　Save what beats there. Filial ingratitude!
　　　Is it not as this mouth should tear this hand
　　　For lifting food to it? But I will punish home!
　　　No, I will weep no more. In such a night
　　　To shut me out! Pour on. I will endure.　　　　　　20
　　　In such a night as this! O Regan, Goneril!
　　　Your old kind father, whose frank heart gave all!
　　　O, that way madness lies. Let me shun that!
　　　No more of that.
KENT: Good my Lord, enter here.
LEAR: Prithee go in thyself. Seek thine own ease.
　　　This tempest will not give me leave to ponder

10. *fixed* – rooted (in the mind)

13. *in the mouth* – face to face
14. *delicate* – sensitive

"This speech marks the turning point of the play, the beginning of Lear's redemption through suffering."
– Isaac Asimov (1920 – 1992), American science and science fiction writer

34. *looped and windowed* – full of holes

35 – 36. *O ...this!* – This is an unusual admission for a king to make. Most members of the nobility in Shakespeare's time were oblivious to the plight of the poor.

36. *Take ... pomp* – "Great vain ones, take medicine to cure yourself."

38. *shake the superflux to* – share your surpluses with

40. This is the cry a sailor would make while testing the water's depth.

On things would hurt me more. But I'll go in.
[To the Fool.] In, boy. Go first. You houseless poverty —
Nay, get thee in. I'll pray, and then I'll sleep.   30

Exit [Fool].

Poor naked wretches, wheresoever you are,
That bide the pelting of this pitiless storm,
How shall your houseless heads and unfed sides,
Your looped and windowed raggedness, defend you
From seasons such as these? O, I have taken
Too little care of this! Take physic, pomp;
Expose thyself to feel what wretches feel,
That thou mayst shake the superflux to them,
And show the heavens more just.
EDGAR: *[Within.]*
Fathom and half, fathom and half! Poor Tom!   40

Enter Fool [from the hovel].

FOOL: Come not in here, Nuncle. Here's a spirit. Help me, help me!
KENT: Give me thy hand. Who's there?
FOOL: A spirit, a spirit! He says his name's poor Tom.
KENT: What art thou that dost grumble there in the straw? Come forth.

Enter Edgar [disguised as a madman].

EDGAR: Away! The foul fiend follows me! Through the sharp hawthorn blows the cold wind. Humh! Go to thy cold bed, and warm thee.
LEAR: Didst thou give all to thy daughters,   50
And art thou come to this?
EDGAR: Who gives anything to poor Tom? Whom the foul fiend hath led through fire and through flame, through ford and whirlpool, over bog and quagmire; that hath laid knives under his pillow and halters in his pew, set ratsbane by his porridge, made him proud of heart, to ride on a bay trotting horse over four-inched bridges, to course his own shadow for a traitor. Bless thy five wits! Tom's a-cold. O, do de, do de, do de. Bless thee from whirlwinds, star-blasting, and taking! Do poor Tom   60
some charity, whom the foul fiend vexes. There could I have him now, and there, and there again, and there!

Storm still.

LEAR: What, have his daughters brought him to this pass?
Couldst thou save nothing? Would'st thou give 'em all?

FOOL: Nay, he reserved a blanket, else we had been all shamed.

LEAR: Now all the plagues that in the pendulous air
Hang fated over men's faults light on thy daughters!

KENT: He hath no daughters, sir.

LEAR: Death, traitor! Nothing could have subdued nature
To such a lowness but his unkind daughters.   70
Is it the fashion that discarded fathers
Should have thus little mercy on their flesh?
Judicious punishment! 'Twas this flesh begot
Those pelican daughters.

EDGAR: Pillicock sat on Pillicock Hill.
'Allow, 'allow, loo, loo!

FOOL: This cold night will turn us all to fools and madmen.

EDGAR: Take heed of the foul fiend. Obey thy parents. Keep
thy word justly. Swear not. Commit not with man's
sworn spouse. Set not thy sweet heart on proud array.   80
Tom's a-cold.

LEAR: What hast thou been?

EDGAR: A servingman, proud in heart and mind, that curled
my hair, wore gloves in my cap, served the lust of my
mistress' heart, and did the act of darkness with her.
Swore as many oaths as I spake words, and broke them
in the sweet face of heaven. One that slept in the
contriving of lust, and waked to do it. Wine loved I
deeply, dice dearly, and in woman out-paramoured the
Turk. False of heart, light of ear, bloody of hand. Hog in   90
sloth, fox in stealth, wolf in greediness, dog in madness,
lion in prey. Let not the creaking of shoes nor the rustling
of silks betray thy poor heart to woman. Keep thy foot
out of brothels, thy hand out of plackets, thy pen from
lenders' books, and defy the foul fiend. Still through the
hawthorn blows the cold wind. Says suum, mun, hey, no,
nonny. Dolphin my boy, boy. Sessa! Let him trot by.

Storm still.

LEAR: Why, thou wert better in thy grave than to answer with
thy uncovered body this extremity of the skies. Is man no
more than this? Consider him well. Thou owest the   100
worm no silk, the beast no hide, the sheep no wool, the
cat no perfume. Ha! Here's three on's are sophisticated!
Thou art the thing itself. Unaccommodated man is no
more but such a poor, bare, forked animal as thou art.
Off, off, you lendings! Come, unbutton here.

---

74. *pelican daughters* –
Pelicans fill their bills with
fish and allow their young to
reach into their mouths to
feed. From a distance,
however, the young pelicans
appear to be striking at the
mother's breast. Hence the
story arose that pelican young
tear at the body of the parent
for sustenance.

78 – 80. Bedlam beggars
used religious language to
keep away any devils that
might wish to possess them.
Here Edgar rephrases some
of the biblical Ten
Commandments.

89 – 90. *out-paramoured the
Turk* – had more lovers than
the sultan of Istanbul

94. *placket* – opening in a
petticoat

98 – 105. Lear reflects on
Tom's nakedness and then
begins to strip away his own
clothing.

103. *unaccommodated* –
without clothes or other
products of civilization

Act Three • Scene 4

FOOL: Prithee, Nuncle, be contented! 'Tis a naughty night to swim in. Now a little fire in a wild field were like an old lecher's heart. A small spark, all the rest on his body cold. Look! Here comes a walking fire.

Enter Gloucester with a torch.

EDGAR: This is the foul fiend Flibbertigibbet. He begins at 110 curfew, and walks till the first cock. He gives the web and the pin, squints the eye, and makes the harelip. Mildews the white wheat, and hurts the poor creature of earth.

> *Swithold footed thrice the old;*
> *He met the night-mare, and her nine fold;*
> *Bid her alight, and her troth plight,*
> *And aroint thee, witch, aroint thee!*

KENT: How fares your Grace?
LEAR: What's he?
KENT: Who's there? What is it you seek? 120
GLOUCESTER: What are you there? Your names?
EDGAR: Poor Tom, that eats the swimming frog, the toad, the tadpole, the wall-newt and the water. That in the fury of his heart, when the foul fiend rages, eats cow-dung for

---

110. *Flibbertigibbet* – One of Shakespeare's contemporaries, Samuel Harsnett, invented a series of devils in his book *Declaration of Egregious Popish Impostures* (1603). Included were Flibbertigibbet, Smulkin, Modo, Mahu, Frateretto, and Hoppedance. Edgar's references here and later in the play to these fiends are consistent with his disguise as Mad Tom.

111. *first cock* – midnight
111 – 112. *web ... pin* – cataract of the eye

sallets, swallows the old rat and the ditch-dog, drinks the green mantle of the standing pool. Who is whipped from tithing to tithing, and stock-punished and imprisoned. Who hath had three suits to his back, six shirts to his body:

> *Horse to ride, and weapons to wear;*
> *But mice and rats, and such small deer,*   130
> *Have been Tom's food for seven long year.*

Beware my follower. Peace, Smulkin! Peace, thou fiend!

GLOUCESTER: What, hath your Grace no better company?

EDGAR: The Prince of Darkness is a gentleman! Modo he's called, and Mahu.

GLOUCESTER: Our flesh and blood, my Lord, is grown so vile, That it doth hate what gets it.

EDGAR: Poor Tom's a-cold.

GLOUCESTER: Go in with me. My duty cannot suffer To obey in all your daughters' hard commands.   140 Though their injunction be to bar my doors And let this tyrannous night take hold upon you, Yet have I ventured to come seek you out And bring you where both fire and food is ready.

LEAR: First let me talk with this philosopher. What is the cause of thunder?

KENT: Good my Lord, take his offer. Go into the house.

LEAR: I'll talk a word with this same learned Theban. What is your study?

125. *sallets* – salads
126. *mantle* – scum; algae
127. *tithing* – a grouping of ten householders; a district

132 – 135. *Smulkin ... Modo ... Mahu* – other names for Harsnett's devils. See note at line 110.

145. *philosopher* – scientist. This meaning explains the subsequent question.

"To see Lear acted, to see an old man tottering about the stage with a walking stick, turned out of doors by his daughters in a rainy night, has nothing in it but what is painful and disgusting. We want to take him into shelter and relieve him. That is all the feeling which the acting of Lear ever produced in me. But the Lear of Shakespeare cannot be acted."
– Charles Lamb (1775 – 1834), English critic and essayist

177. A line from a popular Elizabethan ballad that has not survived.
178. *Fie ... fum* – spoken by the giant in *Jack the Giant-Killer.*

RELATED READING

Calm After Storm – poem by Frank Yerby (page 184)

EDGAR: How to prevent the fiend and to kill vermin.   150
LEAR: Let me ask you one word in private.
KENT: Importune him once more to go, my Lord.
    His wits begin to unsettle.
GLOUCESTER: Canst thou blame him?

Storm still.

His daughters seek his death. Ah, that good Kent!
He said it would be thus, poor banished man!
Thou say'st the King grows mad. I'll tell thee, friend,
I am almost mad myself. I had a son,
Now outlawed from my blood. He sought my life
But lately, very late. I loved him, friend,   160
No father his son dearer. True to tell thee,
The grief hath crazed my wits. What a night is this!
I do beseech your Grace —
LEAR: O, cry you mercy, sir.
    Noble philosopher, your company.
EDGAR: Tom's a-cold.
GLOUCESTER: In, fellow, there, into the hovel. Keep thee warm.
LEAR: Come, let's in all.
KENT: This way, my lord.
LEAR: With him!   170
    I will keep still with my philosopher.
KENT: Good my lord, soothe him. Let him take the fellow.
GLOUCESTER: Take him you on.
KENT: Sirrah, come on. Go along with us.
LEAR: Come, good Athenian.
GLOUCESTER: No words, no words! Hush.
EDGAR: *Child Rowland to the dark tower came,*
    His word was still: Fie, foh, and fum,
    I smell the blood of a British man.

Exeunt.

Act Three
Scene 5

Edmund tells Cornwall about the letter Gloucester has received from France. Cornwall orders Gloucester's arrest and promises to reward Edmund's loyalty by making him Earl of Gloucester.

Gloucester's castle.

Enter Cornwall and Edmund.

CORNWALL: I will have my revenge ere I depart his house.

EDMUND: How, my lord, I may be censured, that nature thus gives way to loyalty, something fears me to think of.

CORNWALL: I now perceive it was not altogether your brother's evil disposition made him seek his death; but a provoking merit, set awork by a reprovable badness in himself.

EDMUND: How malicious is my fortune that I must repent to be just! This is the letter he spoke of, which approves him an intelligent party to the advantages of France. O Heavens! That this treason were not, or not I the detector! 10

CORNWALL: Go with me to the Duchess.

EDMUND: If the matter of this paper be certain, you have mighty business in hand.

CORNWALL: True or false, it hath made thee Earl of Gloucester. Seek out where thy father is, that he may be ready for our apprehension.

EDMUND: *[Aside.]*
If I find him comforting the King, it will stuff his suspicion more fully.

[Aloud to Cornwall.]

I will persever in my course of loyalty, though the conflict be sore between that and my blood. 20

CORNWALL: I will lay trust upon thee, and thou shalt find a dearer father in my love.

Exeunt.

2 – 3. Edmund worries that people will condemn him because he has chosen to be loyal to Cornwall rather than to his own father.

4 – 6. Cornwall believes that Edgar's plot to kill his father was provoked by Gloucester's own evil nature.

8. *just* – virtuous (for revealing his father's treason)

8. *approves* – confirms

9. *advantages* – benefit

17. *comforting* – supporting

19. *persever* – continue; be constant

Act Three
Scene 6

Lear and his company are safe inside a farmhouse. Lear mistakes two stools for Goneril and Regan and puts them on trial for their mistreatment of him. Gloucester brings news that the King's life is in danger and that they must immediately flee to Dover.

A farmhouse near Gloucester's castle.

Enter Gloucester and Kent.

GLOUCESTER: Here is better than the open air. Take it thankfully. I will piece out the comfort with what addition I can. I will not be long from you.

KENT: All the power of his wits have given way to his impatience. The gods reward your kindness!

Exit [Gloucester].
Enter Lear, Edgar, and Fool.

EDGAR: Frateretto calls me, and tells me Nero is an angler in the Lake of Darkness. Pray, innocent, and beware the foul fiend.

FOOL: Prithee, Nuncle, tell me whether a madman be a gentleman or a yeoman.   10

LEAR: A King, a King!

FOOL: No, he's a yeoman that has a gentleman to his son, for he's a mad yeoman that sees his son a gentleman before him.

LEAR: To have a thousand with red burning spits
Come hizzing in upon 'em —

EDGAR: The foul fiend bites my back.

FOOL: He's mad that trusts in the tameness of a wolf, a horse's health, a boy's love, or a whore's oath.

LEAR: It shall be done. I will arraign them straight.   20

[To Edgar.]

Come, sit thou here, most learned justicer.

2. *piece out* – supplement
5. *impatience* – inability to endure more hardships
6. *Frateretto* – another of Harsnett's devils. See note for line 110 of Act Three, Scene 4.
6 – 7. *Nero ... Darkness* – Nero was the notorious Roman emperor who, according to legend, fiddled while Rome burned. The reference to Nero fishing (*angling*) in hell (*the Lake of Darkness*) comes from Chaucer's *The Monk's Tale*.
10. *yeoman* – farmer (just below a gentleman in rank)

15. *red burning spits* – blazing weapons
16. *hizzing* – the sound these weapons make

20. *arraign* – put on trial

21. *justicer* – judge

[To the Fool.]

Thou, sapient sir, sit here. Now, you she-foxes!

EDGAR: Look, where he stands and glares! Want'st thou eyes
at trial, madam?

Come over the bourn, Bessy, to me.

FOOL: *[Sings.]*   *Her boat hath a leak,*
        And she must not speak
    Why she dares not come over to thee!

EDGAR: The foul fiend haunts poor Tom in the voice of a
nightingale. Hoppedance cries in Tom's belly for two   30
white herring. Croak not, black angel. I have no food for
thee.

KENT: How do you, sir? Stand you not so amazed.
Will you lie down and rest upon the cushions?

LEAR: I'll see their trial first. Bring in their evidence.

[To Edgar.]

Thou, robed man of justice, take thy place.

[To the Fool.]

And thou, his yoke-fellow of equity,
Bench by his side.

[To Kent.]

        You are of the commission,
Sit you too.

EDGAR: Let us deal justly.   40

Sleepest or wakest thou, jolly shepherd?
    Thy sheep be in the corn;
And for one blast of thy minikin mouth
    Thy sheep shall take no harm.

Purr, the cat is gray.

LEAR: Arraign her first. 'Tis Goneril. I here take my oath
before this honourable assembly, she kicked the poor
King her father.

FOOL: Come hither, mistress. Is your name Goneril?

LEAR: She cannot deny it.   50

FOOL: Cry you mercy, I took you for a joint-stool.

22. *sapient* – wise
23. *he* – a devil that Edgar claims to see
23. *eyes* – spectators. Edgar offers his imaginary devils as witnesses at the trial.
25. *bourn* – brook. Edgar quotes a line from a long song.

30. *Hoppedance* – another devil

37. *yoke-fellow of equity* – fellow judge

38. *of the commission* – one of the commissioned judges

43. *minikin* – dainty

51. *joint-stool* – low stool with three or four legs

87

52. *warped* – unnatural
53. *store* – material
59 – 60. *My ... counterfeiting* – Lear's madness brings Edgar close to tears. This would give away his disguise (counterfeiting).
63. *Avaunt* – get away
64. *or ... or* – either ... or

67. *brach or lym* – female dog or bloodhound
68. "Either short or long-tailed dog"
71. *hatch* – bottom half of a two-part door
72. *Sessa!* – Off you go!

73. Bedlam beggars carried horns that they would blow as they approached a house. Edgar implies that he is having difficulty maintaining his disguise.

74. *anatomize* – scrutinize closely; dissect

79. *Persian attire* – luxurious clothes. Since Edgar is dressed in rags, Lear's comment is either sarcastic or provides further evidence of his madness.

"So long as hope existed, [the Fool] had sought by his hectic merriment and sarcasms to win Lear back to love and reason ... When all his attempts have failed to soothe ..., he sings in the shivering cold about the necessity of 'going to bed at noon.' He leaves the stage to die in his youth."
– Charles Dickens (1812–1870), English novelist

LEAR: And here's another, whose warped looks proclaim
What store her heart is made on. Stop her there!
Arms, arms, sword, fire! Corruption in the place!
False justicer, why hast thou let her 'scape?
EDGAR: Bless thy five wits!
KENT: O pity! Sir, where is the patience now
That you so oft have boasted to retain?
EDGAR: *[Aside.]*
My tears begin to take his part so much
They'll mar my counterfeiting.   60
LEAR: The little dogs and all,
Tray, Blanch, and Sweetheart, see, they bark at me.
EDGAR: Tom will throw his head at them. Avaunt, you curs!

Be thy mouth or black or white,
Tooth that poisons if it bite;
Mastiff, greyhound, mongrel grim,
Hound or spaniel, brach or lym;
Bobtail tyke or trundle-tail;
Tom will make them weep and wail.
For, with throwing thus my head,   70
Dogs leaped the hatch, and all are fled.

Do de, de, de. Sessa! Come, march to wakes and fairs
and market-towns. Poor Tom, thy horn is dry.
LEAR: Then let them anatomize Regan. See what breeds
about her heart. Is there any cause in nature that makes
these hard hearts?

[To Edgar.]

You, sir, I entertain for one of my hundred. Only I do not
like the fashion of your garments. You will say they are
Persian attire, but let them be changed.
KENT: Now, good my Lord, lie here and rest awhile.   80
LEAR: Make no noise, make no noise. Draw the curtains.
So, so. We'll go to supper in the morning.
FOOL: And I'll go to bed at noon.

Enter Gloucester.

GLOUCESTER: Come hither, friend. Where is the King my
master?
KENT: Here, sir. But trouble him not, his wits are gone.

GLOUCESTER: Good friend, I prithee, take him in thy arms.
I have overheard a plot of death upon him.
There is a litter ready. Lay him in it,
And drive towards Dover, friend, where thou shalt meet   90
Both welcome and protection. Take up thy master.
If thou shouldst dally half an hour, his life,
With thine, and all that offer to defend him,
Stand in assured loss. Take up, take up!
And follow me, that will to some provision
Give thee quick conduct.
KENT: Oppressed nature sleeps.
This rest might yet have balmed thy broken sinews
Which, if convenience will not allow,
Stand in hard cure.   100

[To the Fool.]

                              Come, help to bear thy master.
Thou must not stay behind.
GLOUCESTER: Come, come, away!

Exeunt [all but Edgar].

EDGAR: When we our betters see bearing our woes,
We scarcely think our miseries our foes.
Who alone suffers, suffers most in the mind,
Leaving free things and happy shows behind.
But then the mind much sufferance doth overskip
When grief hath mates, and bearing fellowship.
How light and portable my pain seems now,
When that which makes me bend makes the King bow.   110
He childed as I fathered! Tom, away!
Mark the high noises, and thyself bewray
When false opinion, whose wrong thoughts defile thee,
In thy just proof repeals and reconciles thee.
What will hap more tonight, safe 'scape the King!
Lurk, lurk.

[Exit.]

92. *dally* – delay

98. *balmed ... sinews* –
soothed your shattered nerves
100. *Stand ... cure* – will be
most difficult to cure

RELATED READING

Send in the Clowns –
literary essay by
Goenawan Mohamad
(page 163)

106. *free* – carefree
107. *overskip* – avoid
108. *bearing* – enduring
109. *portable* – endurable

110–111. Edgar recognizes
that he and Lear have
something in common —
family difficulties. Lear has
been abused by his children
and Edgar suffers because of
his father. These lines illus-
trate the parallelism of the
plots of Lear and Edgar.

112. *thyself bewray* – cast
off your disguise
112 – 113. *Mark ... thee* –
Edgar resolves to reveal his
identity when he can provide
proof that he has been falsely
accused.
115. *What ... more* –
whatever else happens
116. *Lurk* – hide

Act Three
Scene 7

Gloucester's castle.

Enter Cornwall, Regan, Goneril, [Edmund the] Bastard, and Servants.

CORNWALL: *[To Goneril.]* Post speedily to my Lord your husband. Show him this letter. The army of France is landed. — Seek out the traitor Gloucester.

[Exeunt some of the Servants.]

REGAN: Hang him instantly.
GONERIL: Pluck out his eyes.
CORNWALL: Leave him to my displeasure. Edmund, keep you our sister company. The revenges we are bound to take upon your traitorous father are not fit for your beholding. Advise the Duke where you are going, to a most festinate preparation. We are bound to the like.   10
Our posts shall be swift and intelligent betwixt us. Farewell, dear sister. Farewell, my Lord of Gloucester.

Enter Oswald.

How now? Where's the King?
OSWALD: My Lord of Gloucester hath conveyed him hence.
Some five or six and thirty of his knights,
Hot questrists after him, met him at gate,
Who, with some other of the lord's dependants,
Are gone with him towards Dover, where they boast
To have well-armed friends.
CORNWALL: Get horses for your mistress.   20
GONERIL: Farewell, sweet Lord, and sister.
CORNWALL: Edmund, farewell.

---

5. Goneril is not present during Gloucester's punishment, but it is her idea to blind him.

RELATED READING

Goneril – short story by Karel Čapek (page 167)

10. *festinate* – urgent
10. *bound to the like* – prepared to do likewise

16. *questrists* – seekers. Shakespeare is credited with coining almost 9000 words. This is one word that did not gain acceptance.

Cornwall and Regan capture Gloucester, interrogate him briefly, and then take out his eyes. Cornwall is injured when an outraged servant attacks him. Regan kills the servant, and the blinded Gloucester is forced to leave his castle and "smell his way to Dover."

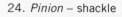

Exeunt Goneril,
[Edmund, and Oswald].

Go seek the traitor Gloucester,
Pinion him like a thief, bring him before us.

[Exeunt other Servants.]

Though well we may not pass upon his life
Without the form of justice, yet our power
Shall do a court'sy to our wrath, which men
May blame, but not control.

Enter Gloucester,
brought in by two or three.

Who's there? the traitor?
REGAN: Ingrateful fox! 'Tis he.   30
CORNWALL: Bind fast his corky arms.
GLOUCESTER: What means, your Graces?
   Good my friends, consider you are my guests.
   Do me no foul play, friends.
CORNWALL: Bind him, I say.

[Servants bind him.]

REGAN: Hard, hard. O filthy traitor!
GLOUCESTER: Unmerciful lady as you are, I am none.
CORNWALL: To this chair bind him. Villain, thou shalt find —

[Regan plucks his beard.]

GLOUCESTER: By the kind gods, 'tis most ignobly done
   To pluck me by the beard.   40
REGAN: So white, and such a traitor!
GLOUCESTER: Naughty lady,
   These hairs which thou dost ravish from my chin
   Will quicken, and accuse thee. I am your host.
   With robber's hands my hospitable favours
   You should not ruffle thus. What will you do?
CORNWALL: Come, sir, what letters had you late from France?
REGAN: Be simple-answered, for we know the truth.
CORNWALL: And what confederacy have you with the traitors
   Late footed in the kingdom?   50
REGAN: To whose hands
   Have you sent the lunatic King? Speak.
GLOUCESTER: I have a letter guessingly set down,

24. *Pinion* – shackle

25. *pass ... life* – pass a
death sentence upon him
27. *do a court'sy* – bend;
give way

31. *corky* – old and withered;
dry

40. *beard* – To the
Elizabethans, a beard was a
sign of manliness and dignity.
To be plucked by the beard
was a terrible insult.

44. *quicken* – come to life

46. *ruffle* – violate

50. *Late footed* – just arrived

53. *guessingly set down* –
with unconfirmed information

60. *Wherefore* – why

63. The Elizabethans enjoyed the violent sport of bear-baiting. Dogs attacked a bear tied to a stake, and the spectators wagered on the results. Gloucester compares himself to the bear and recognizes that he is doomed.

bear-baiting

67. *anointed* – Kings, when crowned, were anointed with holy oil.

69. *buoyed* – risen
70. *stelled fires* – fixed stars
71. *holp* – helped
74. *All ... subscribed* – There is no agreement on the meaning of this line. Shakespearean scholar and editor George I. Duthie says that it may mean: "All other cruel creatures yield to feelings of compassion under strong provocation; you alone do not."
75. *winged* – divine

Which came from one that's of a neutral heart,
And not from one opposed.

CORNWALL: Cunning.

REGAN: And false.

CORNWALL: Where hast thou sent the King?

GLOUCESTER: To Dover.

REGAN: Wherefore to Dover? 60
Wast thou not charged at peril —

CORNWALL: Wherefore to Dover? Let him first answer that.

GLOUCESTER: I am tied to the stake, and I must stand the course.

REGAN: Wherefore to Dover?

GLOUCESTER: Because I would not see thy cruel nails
Pluck out his poor old eyes. Nor thy fierce sister
In his anointed flesh stick boarish fangs.
The sea, with such a storm as his bare head
In hell-black night endured, would have buoyed up
And quenched the stelled fires. 70
Yet, poor old heart, he holp the heavens to rain.
If wolves had at thy gate howled that stern time,
Thou shouldst have said, "Good porter, turn the key."
All cruels else subscribed. But I shall see
The winged vengeance overtake such children.

CORNWALL: See it shalt thou never. Fellows, hold the chair.
Upon these eyes of thine I'll set my foot.

GLOUCESTER: He that will think to live till he be old,
Give me some help!

[Cornwall plucks out one of Gloucester's eyes.]
O cruel! O ye gods!

REGAN: One side will mock another. The other too! 80

CORNWALL: If you see vengeance, —

SERVANT: Hold your hand, my lord!
I have served you ever since I was a child,
But better service have I never done you
Than now to bid you hold.

REGAN: How now, you dog!

SERVANT: If you did wear a beard upon your chin,
I'd shake it on this quarrel.

REGAN: What do you mean?

CORNWALL: My villain! 90

They draw and fight.

SERVANT: Nay, then, come on, and take the chance of anger.

REGAN: *[To another Servant.]*
Give me thy sword. A peasant stand up thus?

She takes a sword and runs at him behind.

SERVANT: O, I am slain! My lord, you have one eye left
    To see some mischief on him. Oh!

He dies.

CORNWALL: Lest it see more, prevent it. Out, vile jelly!
    Where is thy lustre now?
GLOUCESTER: All dark and comfortless! Where's my son
    Edmund?
    Edmund, enkindle all the sparks of nature
    To quit this horrid act.
REGAN: Out, treacherous villain!   100
    Thou call'st on him that hates thee. It was he
    That made the overture of thy treasons to us;
    Who is too good to pity thee.
GLOUCESTER: O my follies! Then Edgar was abused.
    Kind gods, forgive me that, and prosper him!
REGAN: Go thrust him out at gates, and let him smell
    His way to Dover.

Exit [one] with Gloucester.

    How is it, my lord? How look you?
CORNWALL: I have received a hurt. Follow me, lady.
    Turn out that eyeless villain. Throw this slave   110
    Upon the dunghill. Regan, I bleed apace.
    Untimely comes this hurt. Give me your arm.

Exit [Cornwall, led by Regan].

2. SERVANT: I'll never care what wickedness I do,
    If this man come to good.
3. SERVANT: If she live long,
    And in the end meet the old course of death,
    Women will all turn monsters.
2. SERVANT: Let's follow the old Earl, and get the Bedlam
    To lead him where he would. His roguish madness
    Allows itself to anything.   120
3. SERVANT: Go thou. I'll fetch some flax and whites of eggs
    To apply to his bleeding face. Now heaven help him!

Exeunt [severally].

ఎ ఎ ఎ

99. *quit* – requite; repay

102. *overture* – disclosure

104. *abused* – wronged

112. *Untimely* – at the worst time

115 – 117. "Women will all turn into monsters if she lives a long life, because there will be no fear of punishment."
116. *old* – natural
118 – 120. *Bedlam … anything* – Realizing that a Bedlam beggar can help the condemned Gloucester without fear of Cornwall's punishment, the servants agree to place Gloucester in the care of Edgar, who is still in disguise.

Act Three Considerations

ACT THREE Scene 1

▶ Make a list of five plot developments that are discussed in this scene. Based on these developments, what do you predict will become of Lear? What actions might be expected from Goneril, Regan, and their husbands? What role might Cordelia play in subsequent scenes?

ACT THREE Scene 2

▶ In a group, discuss the meaning of one of Lear's speeches in this scene. Prepare a group presentation of the speech. Divide the lines among yourselves and memorize them. When you present the speech to the class, speak the lines expressively. You may wish to use the school's drama room if it is available.

▶ The Fool's prophecy (lines 94–98) contains many statements. What do they have in common? Rewrite the Fool's prophecies using modern details and vocabulary.

ACT THREE Scene 3

▶ What dramatic purposes does this short scene serve?

▶ Based on Edmund's closing speech, what do you predict will happen to Gloucester?

ACT THREE Scene 4

▶ In a few sentences, describe how Lear has changed and speculate on what he might become. Capture the transformation in an alternative title for the play. What speeches in this scene suggest that Lear is undergoing a transformation?

▶ Lear, in his madness, mistakes Tom for a philosopher. Why does Lear think Tom is wise (a learned Theban)?

▶ Irony occurs when language contains two meanings — the meaning the characters perceive, plus the meaning that readers and viewers perceive because they have knowledge that the characters do not possess. This scene, more than most, derives its effectiveness from irony. Reread the scene carefully and compile a list of all the ironies you can find. Compare your list with your classmates'. What do you think are the three greatest ironies? Why?

ACT THREE Scene 5

▶ This scene begins in the middle of a conversation between Cornwall and Edmund. This technique is called *in medias res*, a Latin phrase meaning "in the middle of things." Why is it dramatic in this case to provide only the end of the discussion rather than the whole exchange? Write the dialogue that might have preceded Cornwall's first line.

ACT THREE Scene 6

▶ Look up the words *bathos* and *pathos* and discuss with a partner what they mean. In what way is this scene bathetic? In what way is it pathetic?

▶ The Fool's last words in the play are "And I'll go to bed at noon." Create a journal entry written from the Fool's point of view in which he explains what he means by this line.

▶ Gloucester announces that he has heard of a plot to kill Lear. Who do you think would be behind this plot? What could the plotters gain through Lear's death?

ACT THREE Scene 7

▶ This is one of the most violent scenes in all of Shakespeare's canon, challenging actors and directors who wish to present this scene tastefully and effectively. If you were directing this play, how would you stage the blinding of Gloucester? Work with a group to develop a list of possible approaches.

▶ To reduce the playing time, many directors omit the short exchange between the servants at the end of this scene. Write a paragraph in which you defend or reject the view that this short scene serves an important dramatic function.

Act Four
Scene 1

The heath.

Gloucester, led by an Old Man, meets up with the disguised Edgar. Gloucester convinces Edgar to take him to the cliffs of Dover.

Enter Edgar.

EDGAR: Yet better thus, and known to be contemned,
Than still contemned and flattered. To be worst,
The lowest and most dejected thing of Fortune,
Stands still in esperance, lives not in fear.
The lamentable change is from the best;
The worst returns to laughter. Welcome then,
Thou unsubstantial air that I embrace!
The wretch that thou hast blown unto the worst
Owes nothing to thy blasts.

*Enter Gloucester,
led by an Old Man.*

But who comes here? My father, poorly led?   10
World, world, O world!
But that thy strange mutations make us hate thee,
Life would not yield to age.
OLD MAN: O my good lord,
I have been your tenant, and your father's tenant,
These fourscore years.
GLOUCESTER: Away, get thee away! Good friend, be gone.
Thy comforts can do me no good at all.
Thee they may hurt.
OLD MAN: You cannot see your way.   20
GLOUCESTER: I have no way, and therefore want no eyes.
I stumbled when I saw. Full oft 'tis seen
Our means secure us, and our mere defects
Prove our commodities. Oh dear son Edgar,

1. *contemned* – despised
3. *dejected* – cast down
4. *esperance* – hope
6. *returns to laughter* – changes for the better. Edgar expresses that his miserable situation can only improve.

11 – 13. "O world, it is the unhappy changes and twists of fate that make us hate you and reconcile us to old age (and death)."
16. *fourscore* – eighty
19. "You may be punished for helping me."

21 – 27. Gloucester verbalizes one of the chief paradoxes in the play. When he had eyes, he was blind. Now that he is without eyes, he can see his true son's worth.

23 – 24. *Our ... commodities* – "When all is well, we take things for granted; adversity (defects) proves to be an advantage in forcing us to see life as it really is."

97

25. *food* – object

32 – 33. Edgar now recognizes that someone who can say "This is the worst" still has hope, which means that even worse things are still possible.

37. *reason* – reasoning power; intelligence

43. *wanton* – unrestrained; irresponsible

43 – 44. Gloucester expresses a fatalistic view. British poet William Wordsworth (1770–1850) believed that Shakespeare would not have allowed "any but a heathen character to utter this sentiment." He may be correct since, according to legend, the reign of King Lear took place about eight hundred years before the Common Era.

46. "It is regrettable that I must play the fool in such a sorrowful situation."

47. *Angering* – irritating
51. *overtake* – meet
51. *twain* – two
56. *plague* – curse; sickness
59. *'parel* – apparel; clothing

RELATED READING

The Blind Leading the Blind – poem by Lisel Mueller (page 171)

The food of thy abused father's wrath!
Might I but live to see thee in my touch,
I'd say I had eyes again!

OLD MAN: How now? Who's there?

EDGAR: *[Aside.]*
O gods! Who is it can say "I am at the worst"?
I am worse than ever I was.   30

OLD MAN: 'Tis poor mad Tom.

EDGAR: *[Aside.]*
And worse I may be yet. The worst is not
So long as we can say "This is the worst."

OLD MAN: Fellow, where goest?

GLOUCESTER: Is it a beggarman?

OLD MAN: Madman and beggar too.

GLOUCESTER: He has some reason, else he could not beg.
In the last night's storm I such a fellow saw,
Which made me think a man a worm. My son
Came then into my mind, and yet my mind   40
Was then scarce friends with him.
I have heard more since.
As flies to wanton boys are we to the gods.
They kill us for their sport.

EDGAR: *[Aside.]*
How should this be?
Bad is the trade that must play fool to sorrow,
Angering itself and others.— Bless thee, master!

GLOUCESTER: Is that the naked fellow?

OLD MAN: Ay, my lord.

GLOUCESTER: Then prithee get thee away. If for my sake   50
Thou wilt overtake us, hence a mile or twain
In the way toward Dover, do it for ancient love,
And bring some covering for this naked soul,
Who I'll entreat to lead me.

OLD MAN: Alack, sir, he is mad.

GLOUCESTER: 'Tis the time's plague when madmen lead the
    blind.
Do as I bid thee, or rather do thy pleasure.
Above the rest, be gone.

OLD MAN: I'll bring him the best 'parel that I have,
Come on it what will.   60

Exit.

GLOUCESTER: Sirrah naked fellow —

EDGAR: Poor Tom's a-cold.
     [Aside.]   I cannot daub it further.
GLOUCESTER: Come hither, fellow.
EDGAR: [Aside.]
     And yet I must. —
     Bless thy sweet eyes, they bleed.
GLOUCESTER: Know'st thou the way to Dover?
EDGAR: Both stile and gate, horseway and footpath. Poor Tom
     hath been scared out of his good wits. Bless thee, good
     man's son, from the foul fiend! Five fiends have been in
     poor Tom at once. As Obidicut, of lust. Hoberdidance,   70
     prince of dumbness. Mahu, of stealing. Modo, of
     murder. Flibbertigibbet, of mopping and mowing, who
     since possesses chambermaids and waiting women. So,
     bless thee, master!
GLOUCESTER: Here, take this purse, thou whom the heavens'
          plagues
     Have humbled to all strokes. That I am wretched
     Makes thee the happier. Heavens, deal so still!
     Let the superfluous and lust-dieted man,
     That slaves your ordinance, that will not see
     Because he does not feel, feel your power quickly.   80
     So distribution should undo excess,
     And each man have enough. Dost thou know Dover?
EDGAR: Ay, master.
GLOUCESTER: There is a cliff, whose high and bending head
     Looks fearfully in the confined deep.
     Bring me but to the very brim of it,
     And I'll repair the misery thou dost bear
     With something rich about me. From that place
     I shall no leading need.
EDGAR: Give me thy arm.   90
     Poor Tom shall lead thee.

                    Exeunt.

---

62. *daub it further* – continue with pretending

70 – 72. Edgar names more devils, all from Harsnett. See note for line 110 in Act Three, Scene 4.
72. *mopping and mowing* – grimacing and making faces

78. *superfluous ... man* – pampered man whose desires have been satisfied
79. *slaves ... ordinance* – spurns the law (to share the wealth)

84. *bending* – overhanging
85. *confined deep* – This may be a reference to the Straits of Dover.

Outside Albany's castle, Goneril and Edmund hear from Oswald that the Duke is upset and not acting like his former self. Goneril sends Edmund back to Regan. While Albany rebukes his wife for taking part in driving Lear mad, a Messenger arrives with news of Gloucester's blinding. Albany vows to revenge this foul deed.

1. Even though Goneril and Edmund have been travelling together, the rules of hospitality dictate that she officially welcome him to her castle.

9. *sot* – fool
10. *turned ... out* – had it wrong (in terms of who was loyal and who a traitor)
14. *cowish* – cowardly
15 – 16. *feel ... answer* – react to injuries if this obliges him to retaliate
16 – 17. *Our ... effects* – "The desires we expressed as we travelled together here may come to be." Apparently, Goneril and Edmund have already been plotting against Albany.
17. *my brother* – i.e., Cornwall
18. *musters* – forming an army
19. *change names* – exchange roles
19. *distaff* – a staff used in spinning

Before the Duke of Albany's palace.

Enter Goneril and Edmund.

GONERIL: Welcome, my lord. I marvel our mild husband
Not met us on the way.

Enter Oswald.

Now, where's your master?
OSWALD: Madam, within, but never man so changed.
I told him of the army that was landed.
He smiled at it. I told him you were coming.
His answer was, "The worse." Of Gloucester's treachery
And of the loyal service of his son
When I informed him, then he called me sot
And told me I had turned the wrong side out.   10
What most he should dislike seems pleasant to him.
What like, offensive.
GONERIL: *[To Edmund.]* Then shall you go no further.
It is the cowish terror of his spirit,
That dares not undertake. He'll not feel wrongs
Which tie him to an answer. Our wishes on the way
May prove effects. Back, Edmund, to my brother.
Hasten his musters and conduct his powers.
I must change names at home and give the distaff
Into my husband's hands. This trusty servant   20
Shall pass between us. Ere long you are like to hear

(If you dare venture in your own behalf)
A mistress's command. Wear this. Spare speech.

[Gives a favour.]

Decline your head. This kiss, if it durst speak,
Would stretch thy spirits up into the air.
Conceive, and fare thee well.

EDMUND: Yours in the ranks of death.

Exit.

GONERIL: My most dear Gloucester!
Oh, the difference of man and man!
To thee a woman's services are due.   30
My fool usurps my body.

OSWALD: Madam, here comes my Lord.

Exit [Oswald].
Enter Albany.

GONERIL: I have been worth the whistle.

ALBANY: O Goneril.
You are not worth the dust which the rude wind
Blows in your face! I fear your disposition.
That nature which contemns its origin
Cannot be bordered certain in itself.
She that herself will sliver and disbranch
From her material sap, perforce must wither   40
And come to deadly use.

GONERIL: No more! The text is foolish.

ALBANY: Wisdom and goodness to the vile seem vile.
Filths savour but themselves. What have you done?
Tigers, not daughters, what have you performed?
A father, and a gracious aged man,
Whose reverence even the head-lugged bear would lick,
— Most barbarous, most degenerate — have you madded.
Could my good brother suffer you to do it?
A man, a prince, by him so benefited!   50
If that the heavens do not their visible spirits
Send quickly down to tame these vile offences,
It will come,
Humanity must perforce prey on itself,
Like monsters of the deep.

22. *venture* – act bravely
Stage Direction: *favour* – a love token, perhaps a ring or chain

26. *Conceive* – understand; do your part
31. *fool* – i.e., Cornwall
33. "There was a time when you thought highly enough of me that you would not have delayed in coming to me." *Whistle* refers to an old proverb "It is a poor dog that is not worth the whistling."
36. *disposition* – character
37. *contemns* – despises
38. "Cannot be counted on to restrain itself."
39. *sliver* – tear off

"She that herself will sliver and disbranch"

40. *material sap* – that which gives life and sustenance
41. *deadly use* – be consumed as dry wood in a fire
42. *text* – sermon or teaching
47. *head-lugged* – dragged by the head (therefore annoyed)
48. *madded* – driven to madness
49. *suffer* – allow
51. *visible spirits* – lightning
52. *offences* – offenders
53. "The inevitable will occur"

56. *Milk-livered* – weak and cowardly

57 – 59. Goneril accuses Albany of being weak for turning the other cheek when struck and for not knowing when he has been treated disrespectfully.

63. *helm* – helmet
64. *moral* – moralizing
67. *Proper deformity* – deformity appropriate to a devil

70. *self-covered* – disguised; misleading. Goneril conceals who she really is.
71. *feature* – outward appearance
71. *my fitness* – proper; fitting
74. *However* – but although
75. *shield* – protect
76. "Oh my, what a man!" Goneril mocks Albany's show of manhood.

82. *thrilled* – moved
83. *bending* – wielding
84. *To* – against

89. *nether crimes* – crimes committed below (on Earth)

GONERIL: Milk-livered man!
  That bear'st a cheek for blows, a head for wrongs.
  Who hast not in thy brows an eye discerning
  Thine honour from thy suffering. That not know'st
  Fools do those villains pity who are punished   60
  Ere they have done their mischief. Where's thy drum?
  France spreads his banners in our noiseless land,
  With plumed helm thy state begins to threat,
  Whil'st thou, a moral fool, sits still, and cries
  "Alack, why does he so?"
ALBANY: See thyself, devil!
  Proper deformity seems not in the fiend
  So horrid as in woman.
GONERIL: O vain fool!
ALBANY: Thou changed and self-covered thing, for shame!   70
  Be-monster not thy feature! Were it my fitness
  To let these hands obey my blood,
  They are apt enough to dislocate and tear
  Thy flesh and bones. However thou art a fiend,
  A woman's shape doth shield thee.
GONERIL: Marry, your manhood mew!

Enter a Messenger.

ALBANY: What news?
MESSENGER: O, my good lord, the Duke of Cornwall's dead,
  Slain by his servant, going to put out
  The other eye of Gloucester.   80
ALBANY: Gloucester's eyes?
MESSENGER: A servant that he bred, thrilled with remorse,
  Opposed against the act, bending his sword
  To his great master; who, thereat enraged,
  Flew on him, and amongst them felled him dead.
  But not without that harmful stroke which since
  Hath plucked him after.
ALBANY: This shows you are above,
  You justicers, that these our nether crimes
  So speedily can venge! But, O poor Gloucester!   90
  Lost he his other eye?
MESSENGER: Both, both, my lord.
  This letter, madam, craves a speedy answer.
  'Tis from your sister.

GONERIL: *[Aside.]* One way I like this well.
    But being widow, and my Gloucester with her,
    May all the building in my fancy pluck
    Upon my hateful life. Another way
    The news is not so tart. — I'll read, and answer.

Exit.

ALBANY: Where was his son when they did take his eyes?   100
MESSENGER: Come with my lady hither.
ALBANY: He is not here.
MESSENGER: No, my good lord. I met him back again.
ALBANY: Knows he the wickedness?
MESSENGER: Ay, my good lord. 'Twas he informed against
    him,
    And quit the house on purpose that their punishment
    Might have the freer course.
ALBANY: Gloucester, I live
    To thank thee for the love thou show'dst the King,
    And to revenge thine eyes. Come hither, friend.   110
    Tell me what more thou know'st.

Exeunt.

96 – 98. Goneril is worried that the recently widowed Regan may have a better chance with Edmund. This would destroy her dream *(building in my fancy)* of murdering Albany, marrying Edmund, and becoming ruler of England.

103. *back* – on his way back

"It is one trait of evil that it mistakes goodness for weakness; and Albany becomes all the more detestable to Goneril as she is more and more drawn towards Edmund, a man of her ilk — ungrateful, faithless, and cruel."
– Sarojini Shintri, Indian scholar, Karnatak University

Act Four
Scene 3

Kent, still in disguise, learns from a Gentleman that the King of France has returned home, leaving Cordelia in charge of the French army. The Gentleman describes Cordelia's deep concern for her father, and Kent reveals that Lear is in Dover but refuses to see Cordelia out of shame for the way he treated her.

The French camp near Dover.

Enter Kent and a Gentleman.

3. *imperfect* – unsettled
4. *imports* – bring upon
5. *fear* – panic

9. *pierce* – move

12. *trilled* – trickled

18. *express her goodliest* – make her look more beautiful
20. *a better way* – even more pleasant (than sunshine during rain)
20. *smilets* – little smiles

25. "If it made everyone look as beautiful (as Cordelia)."

KENT: Why the King of France is so suddenly gone back know you the reason?
GENTLEMAN: Something he left imperfect in the state, which since his coming forth is thought of, which imports to the kingdom so much fear and danger that his personal return was most required and necessary.
KENT: Who hath he left behind him general?
GENTLEMAN: The Marshal of France, Monsieur La Far.
KENT: Did your letters pierce the Queen to any demonstration of grief?   10
GENTLEMAN: Ay, sir. She took them, read them in my presence,
And now and then an ample tear trilled down
Her delicate cheek. It seemed she was a queen
Over her passion, who, most rebel-like,
Sought to be king over her.
KENT: O, then it moved her?
GENTLEMAN: Not to a rage. Patience and sorrow strove
Who should express her goodliest. You have seen
Sunshine and rain at once. Her smiles and tears
Were like, a better way. Those happy smilets   20
That played on her ripe lip seemed not to know
What guests were in her eyes, which parted thence
As pearls from diamonds dropped. In brief,
Sorrow would be a rarity most beloved,
If all could so become it.
KENT: Made she no verbal question?

GENTLEMAN: Faith, once or twice she heaved the name of father
　　　Pantingly forth, as if it pressed her heart;
　　　Cried "Sisters, sisters! Shame of ladies! Sisters!
　　　Kent! Father! Sisters! What, in the storm? In the night?　30
　　　Let pity not be believed!" There she shook
　　　The holy water from her heavenly eyes,
　　　And clamour moistened. Then away she started
　　　To deal with grief alone.
KENT: It is the stars,
　　　The stars above us, govern our conditions.
　　　Else one self mate and make could not beget
　　　Such different issues. You spoke not with her since?
GENTLEMAN: No.
KENT: Was this before the King returned?　　　　　40
GENTLEMAN: No, since.
KENT: Well, sir, the poor distressed Lear's in the town.
　　　Who sometime, in his better tune, remembers
　　　What we are come about, and by no means
　　　Will yield to see his daughter.
GENTLEMAN: Why, good sir?
KENT: A sovereign shame so elbows him. His own unkindness,
　　　That stripped her from his benediction, turned her
　　　To foreign casualties, gave her dear rights
　　　To his dog-hearted daughters, these things sting　　　50
　　　His mind so venomously that burning shame
　　　Detains him from Cordelia.
GENTLEMAN: Alack, poor gentleman!
KENT: Of Albany's and Cornwall's powers you heard not?
GENTLEMAN: 'Tis so, they are afoot.
KENT: Well, sir, I'll bring you to our master Lear
　　　And leave you to attend him. Some dear cause
　　　Will in concealment wrap me up awhile.
　　　When I am known aright, you shall not grieve
　　　Lending me this acquaintance. I pray you,　　　60
　　　Go along with me.

Exeunt.

27. *heaved* – uttered with difficulty

33. *clamour moistened* – her grief was accompanied by tears
36. *conditions* – characters
37 – 38. *Else ... issues* – "Otherwise the same husband and wife could not have children that are so different."

43. *better tune* – lucid moments

47. *sovereign* – prevailing
47. *elbows* – pushes him back; reminds him
49. *foreign casualties* – take her chances in foreign lands

57. *dear* – important
59. *aright* – by my true identity (as Kent)
60. *Lending ... acquaintance* – showing me friendship (by confiding in me)

Act Four
Scene 4

Cordelia sends soldiers to look for her father. A Messenger brings word that the British forces are approaching.

The French camp.

Enter, with Drum and Colours, Cordelia, Doctor, and Soldiers.

CORDELIA: Alack, 'tis he! Why, he was met even now
    As mad as the vexed sea, singing aloud,
    Crowned with rank fumiter and furrow-weeds,
    With hardocks, hemlock, nettles, cuckoo-flowers,
    Darnel, and all the idle weeds that grow
    In our sustaining corn. A century send forth.
    Search every acre in the high-grown field
    And bring him to our eye.

    [Exit an Officer.]

                What can man's wisdom
    In the restoring his bereaved sense?
    He that helps him take all my outward worth.   10
DOCTOR: There is means, Madam.
    Our foster-nurse of nature is repose,
    The which he lacks. That to provoke in him
    Are many simples operative, whose power
    Will close the eye of anguish.
CORDELIA: All blessed secrets,
    All you unpublished virtues of the earth,
    Spring with my tears! Be aidant and remediate
    In the good man's distress! Seek, seek for him!
    Lest his ungoverned rage dissolve the life   20
    That wants the means to lead it.

    Enter a Messenger.

2. *vexed* – raging
3 – 6. "All these plants are worthless (*idle weeds*), unlike the *sustaining corn* among which they grow."
6. *century* – a hundred soldiers
8 – 9. *What ... sense* – "What can our knowledge and experience in these matters do to restore his sanity?"
13. *provoke* – induce
14. *simples operative* – effective herbs or medicines
15. "Will cause him to sleep despite his pain."

17. *unpublished ... earth* – Cordelia calls upon the power of white magic, which works through herbs and natural medicines, to heal her father.

18. *aidant and remediate* – helpful and remedial
20. *rage* – madness
21. *wants* – lacks

MESSENGER: News, madam.

    The British powers are marching hitherward.

CORDELIA: 'Tis known before. Our preparation stand

    In expectation of them. O dear father,

    It is thy business that I go about.

    Therefore great France

    My mourning and importuned tears hath pitied.

    No blown ambition doth our arms incite,

    But love, dear love, and our aged father's right.   30

    Soon may I hear and see him!

Exeunt.

28. *importuned* – pleading
29. Cordelia claims that she is not leading her army out of desire for conquest.

Act Four
Scene 5

Gloucester's castle.

Enter Regan and Oswald.

REGAN: But are my brother's powers set forth?
OSWALD: Ay, Madam.
REGAN: Himself in person there?
OSWALD: Madam, with much ado.
    Your sister is the better soldier.
REGAN: Lord Edmund spake not with your Lord at home?
OSWALD: No, Madam.
REGAN: What might import my sister's letter to him?
OSWALD: I know not, Lady.
REGAN: Faith, he is posted hence on serious matter.   10
    It was great ignorance, Gloucester's eyes being out,
    To let him live. Where he arrives he moves
    All hearts against us. Edmund, I think, is gone,
    In pity of his misery, to dispatch
    His nighted life. Moreover, to descry
    The strength of the enemy.
OSWALD: I must needs after him, Madam, with my letter.
REGAN: Our troops set forth tomorrow. Stay with us.
    The ways are dangerous.
OSWALD: I may not, Madam.   20
    My lady charged my duty in this business.
REGAN: Why should she write to Edmund? Might not you
    Transport her purposes by word? Belike,
    Some things — I know not what. I'll love thee much,
    Let me unseal the letter.
OSWALD: Madam, I had rather —

Oswald tells Regan that Goneril and Albany are approaching, but he will not give her the letter he carries from Goneril to Edmund. Regan argues that she has a better claim than Goneril to be Edmund's wife.

1. *brother* – her brother-in-law, Albany

11. *ignorance* – folly; foolish error

15. *nighted* – darkened; blinded
15. *descry* – observe; determine

21. *charged my duty* – insisted that I follow her orders
23. *Belike* – probably

REGAN: I know your Lady does not love her husband.
I am sure of that, and at her late being here
She gave strange oeilliads and most speaking looks
To noble Edmund. I know you are of her bosom.   30

OSWALD: I, Madam?

REGAN: I speak in understanding. Y'are! I know it.
Therefore I do advise you, take this note.
My Lord is dead. Edmund and I have talked,
And more convenient is he for my hand
Than for your Lady's. You may gather more.
If you do find him, pray you give him this.
And when your mistress hears thus much from you,
I pray desire her call her wisdom to her.
So fare you well.   40
If you do chance to hear of that blind traitor,
Preferment falls on him that cuts him off.

OSWALD: Would I could meet him, Madam! I should show
What party I do follow.

REGAN: Fare thee well.

Exeunt.

28. *late* – lately
29. *oeilliads* – winks
30. *of her bosom* – in her confidence
33. *take this note* – take note of this

36. *gather* – guess
37. *this* – It is not clear whether Regan gives Oswald a letter or a token.

42. *Preferment* – advancement
42. *cuts him off* – kills him

Act Four
Scene 6

The country near Dover.

Enter Gloucester,
and Edgar dressed like a peasant.

GLOUCESTER: When shall I come to the top of that same hill?
EDGAR: You do climb up it now. Look how we labour.
GLOUCESTER: Methinks the ground is even.
EDGAR: Horrible steep.
  Hark, do you hear the sea?
GLOUCESTER: No, truly.
EDGAR: Why, then, your other senses grow imperfect
  By your eyes' anguish.
GLOUCESTER: So may it be, indeed.
  Methinks thy voice is altered, and thou speak'st   10
  In better phrase and matter than thou didst.
EDGAR: You're much deceived. In nothing am I changed
  But in my garments.
GLOUCESTER: Methinks you're better spoken.
EDGAR: Come on, sir. Here's the place. Stand still. How fearful
  And dizzy 'tis to cast one's eyes so low!
  The crows and choughs that wing the midway air
  Show scarce so gross as beetles. Halfway down
  Hangs one that gathers sampire, dreadful trade!
  Methinks he seems no bigger than his head.   20
  The fishermen that walk upon the beach
  Appear like mice, and yond tall anchoring bark,
  Diminished to her cock, her cock, a buoy
  Almost too small for sight. The murmuring surge
  That on the unnumbered idle pebble chafes
  Cannot be heard so high. I'll look no more,

8. *anguish* – pain
13. *garments* – Edgar is dressed as a peasant with clothes supplied by the Old Man.
17. *chough* – jackdaw (a variety of crow)

chough

19. *sampire* – herb used in pickling
23. *cock* – cockboat (a small boat)

cockboat

Lest my brain turn, and the deficient sight
Topple down headlong.
GLOUCESTER: Set me where you stand.
EDGAR: Give me your hand. You are now within a foot   30
Of the extreme verge. For all beneath the moon
Would I not leap upright.
GLOUCESTER: Let go my hand.
Here, friend, is another purse. In it a jewel
Well worth a poor man's taking. Fairies and gods
Prosper it with thee! Go thou further off.
Bid me farewell, and let me hear thee going.
EDGAR: Now fare ye well, good sir.
GLOUCESTER: With all my heart.
EDGAR: [Aside.]
Why I do trifle thus with his despair   40
Is done to cure it.
GLOUCESTER: O you mighty gods!

[He kneels.]

This world I do renounce, and, in your sights,
Shake patiently my great affliction off.
If I could bear it longer and not fall
To quarrel with your great opposeless wills,
My snuff and loathed part of nature should
Burn itself out. If Edgar live, O, bless him!
Now, fellow, fare thee well.
EDGAR: Gone, sir, farewell. —   50

*[Gloucester throws himself forward,
as if jumping, and falls.]*

And yet I know not how conceit may rob
The treasury of life when life itself
Yields to the theft. Had he been where he thought,
By this had thought been past. — Alive or dead?
Ho you, sir! Friend! Hear you, sir? Speak! —
Thus might he pass indeed. Yet he revives.
What are you, sir?
GLOUCESTER: Away, and let me die.
EDGAR: Hadst thou been aught but gossamer, feathers, air,
So many fathom down precipitating,   60
Thou'dst shivered like an egg. But thou dost breathe,
Hast heavy substance, bleed'st not, speak'st, art sound.
Ten masts at each make not the altitude

27. *deficient* – failing;
disoriented

35. *Fairies* – It was believed
that fairies guarded hidden
treasures and would reward a
discoverer by making the
treasure multiply.

46. *opposeless* – not to be
challenged
47. *snuff* – candlewick
(i.e., life)

51. *conceit* – imagination

53. *Yields* – gives in; consents

56. *pass* – die

59. *aught* – anything

61. *shivered* – shattered

111

67. *bourn* – boundary; edge (of the sea)

73. *beguile* – cheat

84. *whelked* – twisted

86 – 87. "The pure, bright gods, who deserve to be worshipped because they perform impossible deeds, have saved your life."

"What Edgar says, of course, is literally a lie, although symbolically perfectly true. Gloucester has fallen from an enormous height, he has been led by an evil spirit ... and he has been saved by a miracle — the miraculous devotion of the son he repudiated."
– Phyllis Rackin, American scholar, University of Pennsylvania

Which thou hast perpendicularly fell.
Thy life's a miracle. Speak yet again.
GLOUCESTER: But have I fallen or no?
EDGAR: From the dread summit of this chalky bourn.
Look up a-height. The shrill-gorged lark so far
Cannot be seen or heard. Do but look up.
GLOUCESTER: Alack, I have no eyes!   70
Is wretchedness deprived that benefit
To end itself by death? 'Twas yet some comfort
When misery could beguile the tyrant's rage
And frustrate his proud will.
EDGAR: Give me your arm.
Up. So. How is it? Feel you your legs? You stand.
GLOUCESTER: Too well, too well.
EDGAR: This is above all strangeness.
Upon the crown of the cliff what thing was that
Which parted from you?   80
GLOUCESTER: A poor unfortunate beggar.
EDGAR: As I stood here below, methought his eyes
Were two full moons. He had a thousand noses,
Horns whelked and waved like the enraged sea.
It was some fiend. Therefore, thou happy father,
Think that the clearest gods, who make them honours
Of men's impossibility, have preserved thee.
GLOUCESTER: I do remember now. Henceforth I'll bear

Affliction till it do cry out itself
"Enough, enough," and die. That thing you speak of,   90
I took it for a man. Often 'twould say
"The fiend, the fiend." He led me to that place.

EDGAR: Bear free and patient thoughts.

Enter Lear, mad,
fantastically dressed with weeds.

But who comes here?
The safer sense will never accommodate
His master thus.

LEAR: No, they cannot touch me for coining. I am the King
himself.

EDGAR: O thou side-piercing sight!

LEAR: Nature's above art in that respect. There's your press   100
money. That fellow handles his bow like a crow-keeper.
Draw me a clothier's yard. Look, look, a mouse! Peace,
peace. This piece of toasted cheese will do it. There's my
gauntlet. I'll prove it on a giant. Bring up the brown bills.
O, well flown, bird! In the clout, in the clout! Hewgh!
Give the word.

EDGAR: Sweet marjoram.

LEAR: Pass.

GLOUCESTER: I know that voice.

marjoram

93. *free* – free (from despair); happy

95 – 96. "Only people who are not in their right minds would dress like that."

99. *side-piercing* – heartbreaking

100 – 106. Lear's ravings are directed either at Edgar and Gloucester or at imaginary soldiers. He gives them money and praises their expertise. *Press money* is payment made to persons who have been conscripted into military service; a *clothier's yard* is the length of a typical arrow; *brown bills* are weapons resembling an axe blade on a pole; and *clout* is a reference to the target being aimed at; *hewgh* is the sound that an arrow makes as it flies through the air.

106. *word* – password

107. *marjoram* – herb reputedly effective in treating certain mental illnesses

Act Four • Scene 6

LEAR: Ha! Goneril with a white beard? They flattered me like   110
a dog, and told me I had white hairs in my beard ere the
black ones were there. To say "ay" and "no" to every
thing that I said! "Ay" and "no" too was no good
divinity. When the rain came to wet me once, and the
wind to make me chatter, when the thunder would not
peace at my bidding, there I found them, there I smelt
them out. Go to, they are not men of their words! They
told me I was every thing. 'Tis a lie. I am not ague-proof.

GLOUCESTER: The trick of that voice I do well remember.
Is it not the King?   120

LEAR: Ay, every inch a king.
When I do stare, see how the subject quakes.
I pardon that man's life. What was thy cause?
Adultery? Thou shalt not die. Die for adultery!
No. The wren goes to it, and the small gilded fly
Does lecher in my sight. Let copulation thrive!
For Gloucester's bastard son was kinder to his father
Than my daughters got 'tween the lawful sheets.
To it, luxury, pell-mell! For I lack soldiers.
Behold yond simp'ring dame, whose face between her   130
forks presageth snow, that minces virtue, and does shake
the head to hear of pleasure's name. The fitchew nor the
soiled horse goes to it with a more riotous appetite.
Down from the waist they are Centaurs, though women
all above. But to the girdle do the gods inherit, beneath
is all the fiend's. There's hell, there's darkness, there's the
sulphurous pit — burning, scalding, stench, consump-
tion. Fie, fie, fie! Pah, pah! Give me an ounce of civet,
good apothecary, to sweeten my imagination. There's
money for thee.   140

GLOUCESTER: O, let me kiss that hand!

LEAR: Let me wipe it first. It smells of mortality.

GLOUCESTER: O ruined piece of nature! This great world
Shall so wear out to naught. Dost thou know me?

LEAR: I remember thine eyes well enough. Dost thou squiny
at me? No, do thy worst, blind Cupid! I'll not love. Read
thou this challenge. Mark but the penning of it.

GLOUCESTER: Were all thy letters suns, I could not see one.

EDGAR: [Aside.]
I would not take this from report. It is,
And my heart breaks at it.   150

LEAR: Read.

GLOUCESTER: What, with the case of eyes?

LEAR: O, ho, are you there with me? No eyes in your head, nor no money in your purse? Your eyes are in a heavy case, your purse in a light. Yet you see how this world goes.

GLOUCESTER: I see it feelingly.

LEAR: What, art mad? A man may see how this world goes with no eyes. Look with thine ears. See how yond justice rails upon yond simple thief. Hark in thine ear. Change places and, handy-dandy, which is the justice, which is the thief? Thou hast seen a farmer's dog bark at a beggar?   160

GLOUCESTER: Ay, sir.

LEAR: And the creature run from the cur? There thou mightst behold the great image of authority: a dog's obeyed in office. Thou rascal beadle, hold thy bloody hand! Why dost thou lash that whore? Strip thine own back. Thou hotly lusts to use her in that kind for which thou whipp'st her. The usurer hangs the cozener. Through tattered clothes small vices do appear. Robes and furred gowns hide all. Plate sin with gold, and the strong lance of justice hurtless breaks. Arm it in rags, a pygmy's straw does pierce it. None does offend, none, I say none! I'll able 'em. Take that of me, my friend, who have the power to seal the accuser's lips. Get thee glass eyes and, like a scurvy politician, seem to see the things thou dost not. Now, now, now, now! Pull off my boots. Harder, harder! So.   170

EDGAR: *[Aside.]*
O, matter and impertinency mixed!
Reason, in madness!   180

LEAR: If thou wilt weep my fortunes, take my eyes.
I know thee well enough. Thy name is Gloucester.
Thou must be patient. We came crying hither.
Thou know'st, the first time that we smell the air
We wawl and cry. I will preach to thee. Mark.

GLOUCESTER: Alack, alack the day!

LEAR: When we are born, we cry that we are come
To this great stage of fools. This a good block.
It were a delicate stratagem to shoe
A troop of horse with felt. I'll put it in proof,   190
And when I have stolen upon these sons-in-laws,
Then kill, kill, kill, kill, kill, kill!

Enter a Gentleman with Attendants.

154. *heavy* – sad
155. *light* – empty

161. *handy-dandy* – The challenge in this age-old game is to guess the hand in which an object has been hidden. To trick the other, the person with the object moves it quickly and secretly back and forth between the hands.

167. *beadle* – a minor parish officer who punished petty offenders
169. *kind* – manner
170. *usurer ... cozener* – the moneylender passes judgment on the petty cheat
171. *Robes ... gowns* – clothes associated with judges
174. *it* – sin
174. *able* – vouch for

176. *scurvy* – diseased; vile

179. *matter and impertinency* – common sense and nonsense

183. *came* – were born

185. *wawl* – wail
188. *block* – hat. Perhaps Lear doffs his hat during this speech.
189. *delicate* – clever; neat
190. *put it in proof* – put it to the test

Act Four • Scene 6

200. *seconds* – defenders
201. *salt* – tears

209. *life* – hope
209. *and* – if
210. *Sa ... sa!* – Sounds used
to encourage dogs in the hunt.
It was often used as a cry of
defiance.

211 – 214. In this speech
spoken directly to the audience,
the Gentleman comments on
Lear's plight, which is beyond
words *(Past speaking)*. He also
says that Cordelia's selfless
actions save her from the
condemnation *(general curse)*
inspired by the actions of her
sisters *(twain)*.

216. *speed you* – may you
prosper (a friendly greeting)
217. *toward* – impending
218. *vulgar* – common
knowledge
222 – 223. *The ... thought* –
The main part of the army will
be visible within the hour.

GENTLEMAN: O, here he is! Lay hand upon him. — Sir,
    Your most dear daughter —
LEAR: No rescue? What, a prisoner? I am even
    The natural fool of Fortune. Use me well.
    You shall have ransom. Let me have a surgeon.
    I am cut to the brains.
GENTLEMAN: You shall have anything.
LEAR: No seconds? All myself?   200
    Why, this would make a man a man of salt,
    To use his eyes for garden water-pots,
    Ay, and laying autumn's dust.
GENTLEMAN: Good sir —
LEAR: I will die bravely, like a smug bridegroom. What!
    I will be jovial. Come, come, I am a king.
    My masters, know you that?
GENTLEMAN: You are a royal one, and we obey you.
LEAR: Then there's life in it. Come and you get it, you shall
    get it by running. Sa, sa, sa, sa!   210

Exit running.
[Attendants follow.]

GENTLEMAN: A sight most pitiful in the meanest wretch,
    Past speaking of in a King! Thou hast one daughter
    Who redeems nature from the general curse
    Which twain have brought her to.
EDGAR: Hail, gentle sir.
GENTLEMAN: Sir, speed you. What's your will?
EDGAR: Do you hear aught, sir, of a battle toward?
GENTLEMAN: Most sure and vulgar. Every one hears that
    Which can distinguish sound.
EDGAR: But, by your favour,   220
    How near's the other army?
GENTLEMAN: Near and on speedy foot. The main descry
    Stands on the hourly thought.
EDGAR: I thank you sir. That's all.
GENTLEMAN: Though that the Queen on special cause is here,
    Her army is moved on.
EDGAR: I thank you, sir.

Exit [Gentleman].

GLOUCESTER: You ever-gentle gods, take my breath from me.
    Let not my worser spirit tempt me again
    To die before you please!   230

EDGAR: Well pray you, father.

GLOUCESTER: Now, good sir, what are you?

EDGAR: A most poor man, made tame to Fortune's blows,
Who, by the art of known and feeling sorrows,
Am pregnant to good pity. Give me your hand,
I'll lead you to some biding.

GLOUCESTER: Hearty thanks.
The bounty and the benison of heaven
To boot, and boot!

Enter Oswald.

OSWALD: A proclaimed prize! Most happy!   240
That eyeless head of thine was first framed flesh
To raise my fortunes. Thou old unhappy traitor,
Briefly thyself remember. The sword is out
That must destroy thee.

GLOUCESTER: Now let thy friendly hand
Put strength enough to it.

[Edgar interposes.]

OSWALD: Wherefore, bold peasant,
Dar'st thou support a published traitor? Hence!
Lest that the infection of his fortune take
Like hold on thee. Let go his arm.   250

EDGAR: Chill not let go, zir, without vurther 'casion.

OSWALD: Let go, slave, or thou diest!

EDGAR: Good gentleman, go your gait, and let poor volk
pass. And 'chud ha' bin zwaggered out of my life,
'twould not ha' bin zo long as 'tis by a vortnight. Nay,
come not near th' Old Man. Keep out, che vor' ye, or ise
try whether your costard or my ballow be the harder.
Chill be plain with you.

OSWALD: Out, dunghill!

They fight.

EDGAR: Chill pick your teeth, zir. Come! No matter vor your   260
foins.

[Oswald falls.]

OSWALD: Slave, thou hast slain me. Villain, take my purse.
If ever thou wilt thrive, bury my body,

---

231. *father* – a term of respect. This would not reveal Edgar's identity to Gloucester.
233. *made tame* – humbled and submissive
234 – 235. *Who ... pity* – "Who, having experienced past and present sorrows, is now ready to feel pity for others."
236. *biding* – lodgings
238 – 239. *The ... boot!* – "May you receive the generosity and blessing of heaven as well as my thanks."
240. *proclaimed prize* – According to Regan, Gloucester is a proclaimed traitor and has a price on his head.
243. *thyself remember* – recall your sins and pray for forgiveness
245. *friendly* – Gloucester wishes to die.

248. *published* – publicly proclaimed

251. *Chill* – I will. Edgar puts on a false rustic accent.

256. *che vor' ye* – I warrant you; I assure you
257. *costard* – head (A costard is a type of apple.)
257. *ballow* – staff

261. *foins* – thrusts

And give the letters which thou find'st about me
To Edmund Earl of Gloucester. Seek him out
Upon the British party. O, untimely death! Death!

He dies.

EDGAR: I know thee well. A serviceable villain,
    As duteous to the vices of thy mistress
    As badness would desire.
GLOUCESTER: What, is he dead?   270
EDGAR: Sit you down, father. Rest you.
    Let's see his pockets. These letters that he speaks of
    May be my friends. He's dead. I am only sorry
    He had no other deathsman. Let us see.
    Leave, gentle wax, and, manners, blame us not.
    To know our enemies' minds, we'd rip their hearts;
    Their papers is more lawful.

[Reads the letter.]

    Let our reciprocal vows be remembered. You have
    many opportunities to cut him off. If your will want not,
    time and place will be fruitfully offered. There is nothing   280
    done, if he return the conqueror. Then am I the prisoner,
    and his bed my gaol. From the loathed warmth whereof
    deliver me, and supply the place for your labour.
      Your (wife, so I would say) affectionate servant,
                                Goneril.

O indistinguished space of woman's will!
A plot upon her virtuous husband's life,
And the exchange my brother! Here in the sands
Thee I'll rake up, the post unsanctified
Of murderous lechers. And in the mature time   290
With this ungracious paper strike the sight
Of the death-practised Duke, For him 'tis well
That of thy death and business I can tell.
GLOUCESTER: The King is mad. How stiff is my vile sense,
    That I stand up, and have ingenious feeling
    Of my huge sorrows! Better I were distract.
    So should my thoughts be severed from my griefs,
    And woes by wrong imaginations lose
    The knowledge of themselves.

274. *deathsman* – executioner
275. *Leave* – with your permission
277. *Their papers* – i.e., to rip open their letters

279. *cut him off* – kill him (Albany)

286. *indistinguished ... will* – boundless extent ... lust
288. *exchange* – perhaps, in exchange
289. *rake* – cover. He is covering Oswald, the unholy messenger (*post unsanctified*).
290. *mature* – ripe; right
292. *death-practised* – plotted against
294 – 299. *How ... themselves* – Gloucester envies Lear's insanity because it removes awareness (*ingenious feeling*) of sorrow. Gloucester wishes he were mad (*distract*) so that he could lose consciousness of his griefs.

A drum afar off.

EDGAR: Give me your hand.   300
    Far off, methinks, I hear the beaten drum.
    Come, father, I'll bestow you with a friend.

Exeunt.

Act Four
Scene 7

A Doctor and Cordelia tend the sleeping Lear. When Lear awakes, he is calm and recognizes his daughter. Kent reports that the British forces are rapidly approaching and that the decisive battle will soon be fought.

A tent in the French camp.

Enter Cordelia, Kent, Doctor,
and Gentleman.

CORDELIA: O thou good Kent, how shall I live and work
    To match thy goodness? My life will be too short
    And every measure fail me.
KENT: To be acknowledged, Madam, is overpaid.
    All my reports go with the modest truth,
    No more nor clipped, but so.
CORDELIA: Be better suited.
    These weeds are memories of those worser hours.
    I prithee put them off.
KENT: Pardon, dear Madam.   10
    Yet to be known shortens my made intent.
    My boon I make it that you know me not
    Till time and I think meet.
CORDELIA: Then be it so, my good Lord.
[To the Doctor.] How does the King?
DOCTOR: Madam, sleeps still.
CORDELIA: O you kind gods,
    Cure this great breach in his abused nature!
    The untuned and jarring senses, O, wind up
    Of this child-changed father!   20
DOCTOR: So please your Majesty
    That we may wake the King? He hath slept long.
CORDELIA: Be governed by your knowledge, and proceed
    In the sway of your own will. Is he arrayed?

5. *reports* – i.e., of Lear's madness
6. *clipped* – less
7. *suited* – clothed. Kent is still dressed as a servant.
8. *weeds* – clothes
11. *shortens ... intent* – cuts short my plans
12 – 13. "The only reward I seek is that you not reveal that you know me until a more fitting time."
18. *breach ... nature* – rift in his disturbed mind
19. *wind up* – tune (by tightening the strings)
20. *child-changed* – changed to a child
24. *arrayed* – dressed (like a king)

*Enter Lear in a chair
carried by Servants.*

GENTLEMAN: Ay, madam. In the heaviness of sleep
    We put fresh garments on him.
DOCTOR: Be by, good madam, when we do awake him.
    I doubt not of his temperance.
CORDELIA: Very well.

Music.

DOCTOR: Please you, draw near. Louder the music there!   30
CORDELIA: O my dear father, restoration hang
    Thy medicine on my lips, and let this kiss
    Repair those violent harms that my two sisters
    Have in thy reverence made!
KENT: Kind and dear Princess!
CORDELIA: Had you not been their father, these white flakes
    Did challenge pity of them. Was this a face
    To be opposed against the warring winds?
    To stand against the deep dread-bolted thunder?
    In the most terrible and nimble stroke   40
    Of quick, cross lightning? To watch — poor *perdu!* —
    With this thin helm? Mine enemy's dog,
    Though he had bit me, should have stood that night
    Against my fire. And wast thou fain, poor father,
    To hovel thee with swine and rogues forlorn,
    In short and musty straw? Alack, alack!
    'Tis wonder that thy life and wits at once
    Had not concluded all. He wakes. Speak to him.
DOCTOR: Madam, do you. 'Tis fittest.
CORDELIA: How does my royal Lord? How fares your Majesty? 50
LEAR: You do me wrong to take me out of the grave.
    Thou art a soul in bliss, but I am bound
    Upon a wheel of fire, that mine own tears
    Do scald like molten lead.
CORDELIA: Sir, do you know me?
LEAR: You are a spirit, I know. Where did you die?
CORDELIA: Still, still, far wide!
DOCTOR: He's scarce awake. Let him alone awhile.
LEAR: Where have I been? Where am I? Fair daylight,
    I am mightily abused. I should even die with pity,   60
    To see another thus. I know not what to say.

28. *temperance* – sanity; self-control

"Great poetry is the music by which the cruel truths of life are made tolerable, the means by which they are made into 'the still, sad music of humanity.' *King Lear* is part of that music."
– John M. Lothian, professor, Universities of Saskatchewan and Aberdeen

36. *flakes* – fine hair
37. *Did challenge* – would have claimed
39. *dread-bolted thunder* – dreadful thunderbolts
41. *perdu* – French for "lost one," but here it probably means sentry or guard
42. *helm* – helmet; thin or balding head
44. *fain* – pleased

53. *wheel of fire* – Lear may think he is in hell.

"[Cordelia] is a nurse bestowing the medicine of love upon her patient. She is unconscious of anything else. She has changed from the insolent, wilful girl of Act One who preferred silence to a declaration of love."
– Sophia Blaydes, professor, West Virginia University

60. *abused* – deluded; wronged

I will not swear these are my hands. Let's see.
I feel this pin prick. Would I were assured
Of my condition!

CORDELIA: O, look upon me, sir,
And hold your hand in benediction over me.
No, Sir, you must not kneel.

LEAR: Pray, do not mock me.
I am a very foolish fond old man,
Fourscore and upward, not an hour more nor less; 70
And, to deal plainly,
I fear I am not in my perfect mind.
Methinks I should know you, and know this man.
Yet I am doubtful, for I am mainly ignorant
What place this is, and all the skill I have
Remembers not these garments. Nor I know not
Where I did lodge last night. Do not laugh at me,
For, as I am a man, I think this lady
To be my child Cordelia.

CORDELIA: And so I am! I am! 80

LEAR: Be your tears wet? Yes, faith. I pray, weep not.
If you have poison for me, I will drink it.
I know you do not love me; for your sisters
Have, as I do remember, done me wrong.
You have some cause, they have not.

CORDELIA: No cause, no cause.

LEAR: Am I in France?

KENT: In your own kingdom, Sir.

LEAR: Do not abuse me.

DOCTOR: Be comforted, good Madam. The great rage 90
You see is killed in him. And yet it is danger
To make him even over the time he has lost.
Desire him to go in. Trouble him no more
Till further settling.

CORDELIA: Will it please your Highness walk?

LEAR: You must bear with me.
Pray you now, forget and forgive. I am old and foolish.

Exeunt.
Kent and Attendants [remain].

GENTLEMAN: Holds it true, sir, that the Duke of Cornwall
was so slain?

KENT: Most certain, sir. 100

GENTLEMAN: Who is conductor of his people?

69. *fond* – doting; silly

RELATED READING

Cordelia – literary essay
by Anna Jameson
(page 182)

92. *even over* – fill in

94. *Till ... settling* – until he
is more calm

101. *conductor* – leader

KENT: As 'tis said, the bastard son of Gloucester.

GENTLEMAN: They say Edgar, his banished son, is with the Earl of Kent in Germany.

KENT: Report is changeable. 'Tis time to look about. The powers of the kingdom approach apace.

GENTLEMAN: The arbitrement is like to be bloody. Fare you well, sir.

[Exit.]

KENT: My point and period will be throughly wrought,
Or well or ill, as this day's battle's fought.   110

Exit.

ɘ ɘ ɘ

106. *kingdom* – England
107. *arbitrement* – decisive encounter
109. *point and period* – life's purpose
109. *wrought* – worked out
110. *Or ... or* – Either ... or

Act Four Considerations

ACT FOUR Scene 1

▶ In your own words, explain what Gloucester means by these famous lines, providing evidence from the play upon which Gloucester makes this claim.

> As flies to wanton boys are we to the gods.
> They kill us for their sport (Act Four, Scene 1, lines 43–44).

Still disguised as Tom, Edgar does not reply to Gloucester's statement above. Suppose you are Edgar and wish to reply. Write a short paragraph from Edgar's point of view, exploring whether you agree or disagree with Gloucester's opinion.

▶ Some critics claim that *King Lear* is one of the darkest tragedies ever written because it is bereft of hope. Do you agree with this view, based on what you have read so far? To what extent does Edgar in this scene prove or disprove this opinion?

▶ Write an aside or soliloquy from the point of view of Edgar, in which he reveals why he is taking Gloucester to Dover and what he will do when they arrive. (You will need to make some predictions to complete this assignment.)

ACT FOUR Scene 2

▶ Based on what Albany says and does and on what others say of him, what kind of a person is he? List four character traits, providing evidence from this scene to support each trait.
What role do you think Albany will play in subsequent scenes?

▶ Write a short soliloquy or diary entry in which Goneril reveals her feelings for Edmund and explains how they developed.

▶ Contrast the way in which Goneril and Albany react to the news of Cornwall's death. How may his death complicate the plot?

ACT FOUR Scene 3

▶ This scene does not appear in the Folio edition of the play (see page 9 of the Introduction) and is frequently omitted from stage performances. This scene, however, does serve a number of dramatic purposes. What are they? Consider what new information this scene reveals.

▶ Kent believes in the influence of the stars on human destiny. What rationale does he offer for holding this belief? To what extent do you agree or disagree with him?

ACT FOUR Scene 4

▶ Imagine that you are a journalist assigned to cover the battle between the English and French forces. Having overheard Cordelia's speeches in this scene, write a brief description that captures the most notable aspects of her personality for your readers.

ACT FOUR Scene 5

▶ Write a dialogue between Regan and Oswald (or any other appropriate character) in which Regan clarifies why she wants Gloucester killed.

▶ What does this scene reveal about Oswald?

▶ It appears that both Regan and Goneril want Edmund for a husband. Make two predictions about how this complicated situation will resolve itself.

ACT FOUR Scene 6

▶ Develop one argument that supports the following statement and one argument that disputes it. Consider both the dramatic and thematic purposes for Edgar's behaviours.

> Edgar is justified in hiding his identity from his father and pretending that Gloucester leaped from the cliff.

Which argument do you agree with? Explain why.

▶ This scene marks Lear's first appearance in six scenes. Why might Shakespeare have left Lear off-stage for so long? Consider what dramatic purpose his absence serves.

▶ In this scene, Lear alternates between wisdom and confusion, authority and fragility. Take one of Lear's longer speeches and discuss the different levels of meaning to be found in it.

▶ Write Oswald's obituary. Even a person like Oswald would be treated kindly in an official death announcement. You are welcome to use irony and sarcasm to express your opinion of his character.

ACT FOUR Scene 7

▶ If you were directing this scene, what suggestions would you make to the actor playing Lear? How has Lear's behaviour changed? Why is this change important?

▶ Some critics argue that it is improbable that Cordelia would forgive Lear for what he did. Do you agree? Write a defence or criticism of Shakespeare's characterization of Cordelia in this scene.

Act Five
Scene 1

The British camp near Dover.

To deal with Cordelia's army, Albany joins forces with Edmund and Regan. Edgar, still in disguise, gives Albany the letter he found on Oswald's body and claims he knows someone who will challenge Edmund. Edmund reveals his plan to become sole ruler of England by arranging the deaths of Albany, Lear, and Cordelia.

Enter, with Drum and Colours,
Edmund, Regan, Gentleman,
and Soldiers.

EDMUND: Know of the Duke if his last purpose hold,
Or whether since he is advised by aught
To change the course. He's full of alteration
And self-reproving. Bring his constant pleasure.

[Exit an Officer.]

REGAN: Our sister's man is certainly miscarried.
EDMUND: 'Tis to be doubted, Madam.
REGAN: Now, sweet lord,
You know the goodness I intend upon you.
Tell me, but truly, but then speak the truth,
Do you not love my sister?   10
EDMUND: In honoured love.
REGAN: But have you never found my brother's way
To the forfended place?
EDMUND: That thought abuses you.
REGAN: I am doubtful that you have been conjunct
And bosomed with her, as far as we call hers.
EDMUND: No, by mine honour, Madam.
REGAN: I never shall endure her. Dear my lord,
Be not familiar with her.
EDMUND: Fear me not.   20
She and the Duke her husband!

1 – 3. *Know ... course* – Edmund wants to know if Albany is still prepared to fight or if he has changed his mind.
3. *alteration* – indecision
4. *constant pleasure* – final decision
5. *sister's man* – Oswald
5. *miscarried* – come to harm
6. *doubted* – suspected

13. *forfended* – forbidden (i.e., Goneril's bed)
14. *abuses* – is not worthy of
15. *am doubtful* – suspect
15. *conjunct* – in league with
16. *as ... hers* – in the fullest sense

Act Five • Scene 1

Enter, with Drum and Colours,
Albany, Goneril, and Soldiers.

GONERIL: *[Aside.]*
    I had rather lose the battle than that sister
    Should loosen him and me.
ALBANY: Our very loving sister, well be-met.
    Sir, this I hear: the King is come to his daughter,
    With others whom the rigour of our state
    Forced to cry out. Where I could not be honest,
    I never yet was valiant. For this business,
    It touches us as France invades our land,
    Not bolds the King, with others whom, I fear,   30
    Most just and heavy causes make oppose.
EDMUND: Sir, you speak nobly.
REGAN: Why is this reasoned?
GONERIL: Combine together 'gainst the enemy.
    For these domestic and particular broils
    Are not the question here.
ALBANY: Let's then determine
    With the ancient of war on our proceeding.
EDMUND: I shall attend you presently at your tent.
REGAN: Sister, you'll go with us?   40
GONERIL: No.
REGAN: 'Tis most convenient. Pray go with us.
GONERIL: *[Aside.]*
    O, ho, I know the riddle. I will go.

As they are going out, enter Edgar, disguised.

EDGAR: If ever your Grace had speech with man so poor,
    Hear me one word.
ALBANY: *[To those who are leaving.]*
    I'll overtake you.

Exeunt [all but Albany and Edgar].

                  Speak.
EDGAR: Before you fight the battle, ope this letter.
    If you have victory, let the trumpet sound
    For him that brought it. Wretched though I seem,
    I can produce a champion that will prove   50
    What is avouched there. If you miscarry,
    Your business of the world hath so an end,
    And machination ceases. Fortune love you!

26. *rigour ... state* – severity of our rule

30. *Not ... King* – "Not because it emboldens the King"
32. *nobly* – Edmund likely is speaking sarcastically
33. *reasoned* – mentioned
34. *Combine together* – join forces
35. *particular broils* – personal quarrels
38. *ancient* – most experienced

42. *convenient* – proper; fitting

46. *overtake* – catch up to

51. *avouched* – attested to; claimed
51. *miscarry* – lose
53. *machination* – treachery

ALBANY: Stay till I have read the letter.
EDGAR: I was forbid it.
When time shall serve, let but the herald cry,
And I'll appear again.
ALBANY: Why, fare thee well. I will overlook thy paper.

Exit [Edgar]. Enter Edmund.

EDMUND: The enemy is in view. Draw up your powers.
Here is the guess of their true strength and forces   60
By diligent discovery. But your haste
Is now urged on you.
ALBANY: We will greet the time.

Exit.

EDMUND: To both these sisters have I sworn my love.
Each jealous of the other, as the stung
Are of the adder. Which of them shall I take?
Both? One? Or neither? Neither can be enjoyed,
If both remain alive. To take the widow
Exasperates, makes mad her sister Goneril.
And hardly shall I carry out my side,   70
Her husband being alive. Now then, we'll use
His countenance for the battle, which being done,
Let her who would be rid of him devise
His speedy taking off. As for the mercy
Which he intends to Lear and to Cordelia,
The battle done, and they within our power,
Shall never see his pardon. For my state
Stands on me to defend, not to debate.

Exit.

61. *discovery* – scouting; spying

65. *jealous* – suspicious
66. *adder* – poisonous snake

70. "And with difficulty will my plan succeed"
72. *countenance* – authority
74. *taking off* – murder
77. *state* – Edmund wants to be king, which necessitates the death of Lear and Cordelia.

"On the whole, and this is true of other plays besides *King Lear*, Shakespeare tends to give more intellectual ability to his sinners than to his saints. Edmund, for instance, is so shrewd and witty that he almost wins our sympathy for his unabashed cruelty."
– Enid Welsford, English scholar

Act Five
Scene 2

Cordelia's army prepares for battle. Edgar hides his father and then joins the battle. He returns quickly from battle with news that the French forces have been defeated and that Cordelia and Lear have been captured.

A field between the two camps.

*Alarum within. Enter, with Drum and Colours,
Lear, Cordelia, and soldiers,
and exeunt.*

Enter Edgar and Gloucester.

EDGAR: Here, father, take the shadow of this tree
For your good host. Pray that the right may thrive.
If ever I return to you again,
I'll bring you comfort.
GLOUCESTER: Grace go with you, sir!

*Exit [Edgar].
Alarum and retreat within.
Enter Edgar.*

EDGAR: Away, old man! give me thy hand! Away!
King Lear hath lost, he and his daughter taken.
Give me thy hand! Come on!
GLOUCESTER: No further, sir. A man may rot even here.
EDGAR: What, in ill thoughts again? Men must endure   10
Their going hence, even as their coming hither.
Ripeness is all. Come on.
GLOUCESTER: And that's true too.

Exeunt.

---

2. *host* – shelter

12. *Ripeness is all* – Edgar says that death cannot be avoided and that all one can hope for is to be ready for it. Hamlet expresses a similar view: "The readiness is all" (Act Five, Scene 2, line 219). Edgar suggests that not only are we born in pain but we should also expect to suffer *(endure)* when we die.

"The spirit gone, man is garbage ... Ripeness was all."
– Joseph Heller (b. 1923), American novelist

Act Five
Scene 3

The British camp near Dover.

Enter, in conquest, with Drum and Colours, Edmund;
Lear and Cordelia as prisoners;
Soldiers, Captain.

EDMUND: Some officers take them away. Good guard
　　　　Until their greater pleasures first be known
　　　　That are to censure them.
CORDELIA: We are not the first
　　　　Who with best meaning have incurred the worst.
　　　　For thee, oppressed King, am I cast down.
　　　　Myself could else out-frown false Fortune's frown.
　　　　Shall we not see these daughters and these sisters?
LEAR: No, no, no, no! Come, let's away to prison.
　　　　We two alone will sing like birds in the cage.　　　　10
　　　　When thou dost ask me blessing, I'll kneel down
　　　　And ask of thee forgiveness. So we'll live,
　　　　And pray, and sing, and tell old tales, and laugh
　　　　At gilded butterflies, and hear poor rogues
　　　　Talk of court news. And we'll talk with them too,
　　　　Who loses and who wins. Who's in, who's out,
　　　　And take upon us the mystery of things,
　　　　As if we were God's spies. And we'll wear out,
　　　　In a walled prison, packs and sects of great ones
　　　　That ebb and flow by the moon.　　　　20
EDMUND: Take them away.
LEAR: Upon such sacrifices, my Cordelia,
　　　　The gods themselves throw incense. Have I caught thee?
　　　　He that parts us shall bring a brand from heaven
　　　　And fire us hence like foxes. Wipe thine eyes.

The battle over, Edmund sends Lear and Cordelia to prison under guard, and secretly orders a Captain to kill them both. Albany accuses Edmund and Goneril of treason. Regan announces that she and Edmund will be married, but is poisoned by Goneril, who later kills herself. Summoned by a herald, Edgar engages Edmund in a duel and fatally wounds him. It is revealed that Gloucester has died, and Lear carries in Cordelia's body, and then also dies. Albany resigns his power, leaving Edgar to rule England.

2. *greater pleasures* – the desires of those higher in rank
3. *censure* – judge
7. *else* – otherwise
14. *gilded butterflies* – brightly dressed courtiers
17. *take ... things* – talk as if we understand the world's mysteries
18. *wear out* – outlive
19. *packs and sects* – groups and factions
20. *ebb and flow* – come in and out of favour
22. *sacrifices* – Lear could be referring to his and Cordelia's imprisonment or to Cordelia's return to England to support Lear.
24 – 25. Lear suggests that only heavenly powers could part him and Cordelia. Elizabethans smoked foxes out of their holes with fire.

26. *goodyears* – evil forces such as plagues or pestilence
26. *fell* – skin

The goodyears shall devour them, flesh and fell,
Ere they shall make us weep! We'll see them starved first.
Come.

Exeunt [Lear and Cordelia, guarded].

EDMUND: Come hither, Captain. Hark.
Take thou this note.

[Gives a paper].

30. *note* – orders for the execution of Lear and Cordelia
33 – 34. *men ... is* – In times of peace, one can be merciful; in times of war, one must be ruthless.
35 – 36. *Thy ... question* – Your important task must not be discussed.
39. *write happy* – consider yourself lucky

42. "I am not a horse or beast of burden."

      Go follow them to prison.   30
One step I have advanced thee. If thou dost
As this instructs thee, thou dost make thy way
To noble fortunes. Know thou this, that men
Are as the time is. To be tender-minded
Does not become a sword. Thy great employment
Will not bear question. Either say thou'lt do it,
Or thrive by other means.
CAPTAIN: I'll do it, my lord.
EDMUND: About it! And write happy when thou hast done.
 Mark, — I say, instantly, and carry it so 40
 As I have set it down.
CAPTAIN: I cannot draw a cart, nor eat dried oats.
 If it be man's work, I'll do it.

Exit.

Flourish.
Enter Albany, Goneril, Regan, Soldiers.

46. *opposites* – opponents

ALBANY: Sir, you have showed today your valiant strain,
 And Fortune led you well. You have the captives
 Who were the opposites of this day's strife.
 We do require them of you, so to use them
 As we shall find their merits and our safety
 May equally determine.
EDMUND: Sir, I thought it fit 50
 To send the old and miserable King

52. *retention* – imprisonment
54 – 56. "To win the hearts of the people and turn our own conscripted soldiers against us."

 To some retention and appointed guard.
 Whose age has charms in it, whose title more,
 To pluck the common bosom on his side
 And turn our impressed lances in our eyes
 Which do command them. With him I sent the Queen,
 My reason all the same. And they are ready

Tomorrow, or at further space, to appear
Where you shall hold your session. At this time
We sweat and bleed. The friend hath lost his friend,   60
And the best quarrels, in the heat, are cursed
By those that feel their sharpness.
The question of Cordelia and her father
Requires a fitter place.
ALBANY: Sir, by your patience,
I hold you but a subject of this war,
Not as a brother.
REGAN: That's as we list to grace him.
Methinks our pleasure might have been demanded
Ere you had spoke so far. He led our powers,   70
Bore the commission of my place and person,
The which immediacy may well stand up
And call itself your brother.
GONERIL: Not so hot!
In his own grace he doth exalt himself
More than in your addition.
REGAN: In my rights,
By me invested, he compeers the best.
GONERIL: That were the most if he should husband you.
REGAN: Jesters do oft prove prophets.   80
GONERIL: Holla, holla!
That eye that told you so looked but a-squint.
REGAN: Lady, I am not well, else I should answer
From a full-flowing stomach.

[To Edmund.]

General,
Take thou my soldiers, prisoners, patrimony;
Dispose of them, of me. The walls are thine.
Witness the world that I create thee here
My lord and master.
GONERIL: Mean you to enjoy him?
ALBANY: The let-alone lies not in your good will.   90
EDMUND: Nor in thine, lord.
ALBANY: Half-blooded fellow, yes.
REGAN: *[To Edmund.]*
Let the drum strike, and prove my title thine.
ALBANY: Stay yet. Hear reason. Edmund, I arrest thee
On capital treason. And, in thy attaint,

[Points to Goneril.]

61. *in the heat* – i.e., of passion

68. *list* – desire

72. *immediacy* – immediate connection (to me)

76. *your addition* – titles that you have conferred on him
78. *compeers* – is a peer or equal to

81. *Holla* – hello
82. *a-squint* – cross-eyed (i.e., wrongly)
84. *stomach* – i.e., anger

85. *patrimony* – inheritance

90. *let-alone* – permission

92. *Half-blooded* – illegitimate

95. *in thy attaint* – as your (corrupted) accomplice

98. *subcontracted* – engaged.
Albany is speaking
sarcastically.
99. *banes* – banns; wedding
announcement

101. *bespoke* – spoken for
102. *interlude* – farcical
entertainment

105. *heinous* – evil
106. *pledge* – challenge
106. *make* – prove

110. *medicine* – poison.
Goneril has poisoned her
sister.

117. *virtue* – strength
119. *Took ... discharge* – have
been dismissed
120. *grows upon* – overcomes

This gilded serpent.

[To Regan.]   For your claim, fair sister,
I bar it in the interest of my wife.
'Tis she is subcontracted to this lord,
And I, her husband, contradict your banes.
If you will marry, make your loves to me;   100
My lady is bespoke.
GONERIL: An interlude!
ALBANY: Thou art armed, Gloucester. Let the trumpet sound.
If none appear to prove upon thy person
Thy heinous, manifest, and many treasons,
There is my pledge!

[Throws down a glove.]

           I'll make it on thy heart,
Ere I taste bread, thou art in nothing less
Than I have here proclaimed thee.
REGAN: Sick! O, sick!
GONERIL: *[Aside.]*
If not, I'll never trust medicine.   110
EDMUND: There's my exchange.

[Throws down a glove.]

        What in the world he is
That names me traitor, villain-like he lies.
Call by thy trumpet. He that dares approach,
On him, on you, who not? I will maintain
My truth and honour firmly.
ALBANY: A herald, ho!
Trust to thy single virtue. For thy soldiers,
All levied in my name, have in my name
Took their discharge.
REGAN: My sickness grows upon me.   120
ALBANY: She is not well. Convey her to my tent.

[Exit Regan, led.]
Enter a Herald.

Come hither, herald. Let the trumpet sound,
And read out this.
OFFICER: Sound, trumpet!

A trumpet sounds.

HERALD: *[Reads.]* *If any man of quality or degree within the lists of the army will maintain upon Edmund, supposed Earl of Gloucester, that he is a manifold traitor, let him appear by the third sound of the trumpet. He is bold in his defence.*

Sound!   *First trumpet.*   130

Again!   *Second trumpet.*

Again!   *Third trumpet.*

Trumpet answers within.
Enter Edgar, armed, with a trumpet before him.

ALBANY: Ask him his purposes, why he appears
   Upon this call of the trumpet.
HERALD: What are you?
   Your name, your quality? And why you answer
   This present summons?
EDGAR: Know my name is lost.
   By treason's tooth bare-gnawn and canker-bit.
   Yet am I noble as the adversary   140
   I come to cope.
ALBANY: Which is that adversary?
EDGAR: What's he that speaks for Edmund Earl of Gloucester?
EDMUND: Himself. What say'st thou to him?
EDGAR: Draw thy sword,
   That, if my speech offend a noble heart,
   Thy arm may do thee justice. Here is mine.
   Behold, it is the privilege of mine honours,
   My oath, and my profession. I protest,
   Maugre thy strength, youth, place, and eminence,   150
   Despite thy victor sword and fire-new fortune,
   Thy valour and thy heart, thou art a traitor,
   False to thy gods, thy brother, and thy father,
   Conspirant 'gainst this high illustrious prince,
   And from the extremest upward of thy head
   To the descent and dust beneath thy foot,
   A most toad-spotted traitor. Say thou "No,"
   This sword, this arm, and my best spirits are bent
   To prove upon thy heart, whereto I speak,
   Thou liest.   160

125. *quality* – rank

139. *bare-gnawn ... canker-bit* – bare and withered
141. *cope* – face; encounter

145 – 149. Edgar claims the right, because of his rank as a knight, to challenge Edmund.

150. *Maugre* – in spite of
151. *fire-new* – fresh; brand new

135

161. *In wisdom* – Because
Edmund is not compelled to
fight one of lower rank, he
would be wise to determine
his opponent's identity before
risking his life.

164. *safe and nicely* – legally

168. *for* – since

169. *way* – entrance (into
your heart)

171. *Save him* – Edmund
has been wounded. However,
Albany wants him to live so
that he can force a
confession from him.

172. *practice* – treachery

175. *cozened and beguiled* –
cheated and tricked

182. *arraign* – formally
charge

191. *charity* – forgiveness
192. *blood* – nobility
195. *pleasant vices* –
adultery

EDMUND: In wisdom I should ask thy name,
But since thy outside looks so fair and warlike,
And that thy tongue some say of breeding breathes,
What safe and nicely I might well delay
By rule of knighthood, I disdain and spurn.
Back do I toss those treasons to thy head,
With the hell-hated lie overwhelm thy heart,
Which, for they yet glance by and scarcely bruise,
This sword of mine shall give them instant way,
Where they shall rest for ever. Trumpets, speak!   170

Alarums. They fight.
[Edmund falls.]

ALBANY: Save him, save him!
GONERIL: This is mere practice, Gloucester.
By the law of arms thou wast not bound to answer
An unknown opposite. Thou art not vanquished,
But cozened and beguiled.
ALBANY: Shut your mouth, dame,
Or with this paper shall I stop it.
[To Edmund.] Hold, sir.
[To Goneril.] Thou worse than any name, read thine own evil.
No tearing, lady! I perceive you know it.   180
GONERIL: Say if I do, the laws are mine, not thine.
Who can arraign me for it?
ALBANY: Most monstrous! O know'st thou this paper?
GONERIL: Ask me not what I know.

Exit.

ALBANY: Go after her. She's desperate. Govern her.

[Exit an Officer.]

EDMUND: What you have charged me with, that have I done,
And more, much more. The time will bring it out.
'Tis past, and so am I. But what art thou
That hast this fortune on me? If thou art noble,
I do forgive thee.   190
EDGAR: Let's exchange charity.
I am no less in blood than thou art, Edmund.
If more, the more thou hast wronged me.
My name is Edgar, and thy father's son.
The gods are just, and of our pleasant vices

Act Five • Scene 3

Make instruments to plague us.
The dark and vicious place where thee he got
Cost him his eyes.

EDMUND: Thou hast spoken right. 'Tis true.
The wheel is come full circle. I am here.   200

ALBANY: Methought thy very gait did prophesy
A royal nobleness. I must embrace thee.
Let sorrow split my heart if ever I
Did hate thee, or thy father!

EDGAR: Worthy prince, I know it.

ALBANY: Where have you hid yourself?
How have you known the miseries of your father?

EDGAR: By nursing them, my lord. List a brief tale,
And when 'tis told, O that my heart would burst!
The bloody proclamation to escape   210
That followed me so near, — O, our lives' sweetness!
That with the pain of death would hourly die
Rather than die at once! — taught me to shift
Into a madman's rags, to assume a semblance
That very dogs disdained; and in this habit
Met I my father with his bleeding rings,
Their precious stones new lost, became his guide,
Led him, begged for him, saved him from despair.
Never — O fault! — revealed myself unto him
Until some half hour past, when I was armed,   220
Not sure, though hoping of this good success,
I asked his blessing, and from first to last
Told him my pilgrimage. But his flawed heart —
Alack, too weak the conflict to support —
'Twixt two extremes of passion, joy and grief,
Burst smilingly.

EDMUND: This speech of yours hath moved me,
And shall perchance do good. But speak you on.
You look as you had something more to say.

ALBANY: If there be more, more woeful, hold it in,   230
For I am almost ready to dissolve,
Hearing of this.

EDGAR: This would have seemed a period
To such as love not sorrow. But another,
To amplify too much, would make much more,
And top extremity.
Whilst I was big in clamour, came there a man,
Who, having seen me in my worst estate,
Shunned my abhorred society; but then, finding
Who 'twas that so endured, with his strong arms   240

196. *instruments* – illegitimate offspring

200. *wheel* – the wheel of Fortune
201. *gait* – bearing; manner of walking

208. *List* – listen to
211 – 213. *O … once* – "We value the sweetness of life so much that we would rather suffer hour after hour than die at once."
213. *shift* – change
215. *habit* – disguise; appearance
216. *rings* – (eye) sockets

223. *flawed* – cracked

231. *dissolve* – weep

233. *period* – end; limit

236. *top extremity* – exceed the extreme limits (of sorrow)
237. *clamour* – sorrow; lamentation
238. *estate* – condition (disguised as Tom O'Bedlam)

242. *As* – as if
242. *him* – himself
245. *puissant* – powerful

245 – 247. Kent is only forty-eight, but in Shakespeare's day he would have been considered old. From Edgar's account, it appears that Kent is dying.

247. *tranced* – unconscious
250. *enemy* – hostile (Lear considered Kent to be an enemy.)
251. *for* – even for

267. *compliment* – ceremony
268. *manners* – politeness
270. *aye* – forever

"This amnesia on everybody's part is necessary for the climax that follows, but — though the audience thinks little of it — the reader always feels a shock."
– G.L. Kittredge (1860 – 1941), American scholar

274. *object* – sight

He fastened on my neck, and bellowed out
As he'd burst heaven. Threw him on my father;
Told the most piteous tale of Lear and him
That ever ear received. Which in recounting
His grief grew puissant, and the strings of life
Began to crack. Twice then the trumpets sounded,
And there I left him tranced.
ALBANY: But who was this?
EDGAR: Kent, sir, the banished Kent; who in disguise
Followed his enemy king and did him service   250
Improper for a slave.

Enter a Gentleman with a bloody knife.

GENTLEMAN: Help, help! O, help!
EDGAR: What kind of help?
ALBANY: Speak, man.
EDGAR: What means that bloody knife?
GENTLEMAN: 'Tis hot, it smokes.
It came even from the heart of — O! She's dead!
ALBANY: Who dead? Speak, man.
GENTLEMAN: Your lady, sir, your lady! And her sister
By her is poisoned. She confesses it.   260
EDMUND: I was contracted to them both. All three
Now marry in an instant.

Enter Kent.

EDGAR: Here comes Kent.
ALBANY: Produce their bodies, be they alive or dead.

[Exit Gentleman.]

This judgement of the heavens, that makes us tremble
Touches us not with pity. O, is this he?
The time will not allow the compliment
That very manners urges.
KENT: I am come
To bid my king and master aye good night.   270
Is he not here?
ALBANY: Great thing of us forgot!
Speak, Edmund, where's the King? And where's Cordelia?

The bodies of Goneril and Regan are brought in.
[Albany points to the bodies.]

Seest thou this object, Kent?

KENT: Alack, why thus?
EDMUND: Yet Edmund was beloved.
 The one the other poisoned for my sake,
 And after slew herself.
ALBANY: Even so. Cover their faces.
EDMUND: I pant for life. Some good I mean to do,   280
 Despite of mine own nature. Quickly send —
 Be brief in't — to the castle. For my writ
 Is on the life of Lear and on Cordelia.
 Nay, send in time.
ALBANY: Run, run, O, run!
EDGAR: To who, my lord? Who has the office? Send
 Thy token of reprieve.
EDMUND: Well thought on. Take my sword,
 Give it the Captain.
EDGAR: Haste thee for thy life.   290

[Exit Officer.]

EDMUND: He hath commission from thy wife and me
 To hang Cordelia in the prison and
 To lay the blame upon her own despair
 That she fordid herself.
ALBANY: The gods defend her! Bear him hence awhile.

[Edmund is borne off.]
Enter Lear, with Cordelia [dead] in his arms
[Edgar, Captain, and others following].

LEAR: Howl, howl, howl! O, you are men of stone.
 Had I your tongues and eyes, I'd use them so
 That heaven's vault should crack. She's gone for ever!
 I know when one is dead, and when one lives.
 She's dead as earth. Lend me a looking glass.   300
 If that her breath will mist or stain the stone,
 Why, then she lives.
KENT: Is this the promised end?
EDGAR: Or image of that horror?
ALBANY: Fall and cease!
LEAR: This feather stirs. She lives! If it be so,
 It is a chance which does redeem all sorrows
 That ever I have felt.
KENT: O my good master!
LEAR: Prithee away!   310
EDGAR: 'Tis noble Kent, your friend.

"*[King Lear]* asks abstract, unanswerable questions, but it addresses real and enduring problems: aging parents, sibling rivalries, the relationship between father and child, the social problems of homelessness, and how easy it is to ignore suffering — when it happens to others."
– Norrie Epstein, American professor, University of California

294. *fordid* – killed

300. *looking glass* – small mirror

303. *promised end* – the end of the world; the day of judgment
305. "Let heaven fall and everything cease!"

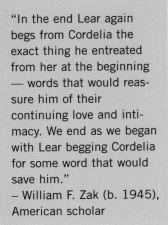

"In the end Lear again begs from Cordelia the exact thing he entreated from her at the beginning — words that would reassure him of their continuing love and intimacy. We end as we began with Lear begging Cordelia for some word that would save him."
– William F. Zak (b. 1945), American scholar

320. *falchion* – sharp light sword

falchion

322. *crosses* – sword parries; also troubles
325. *One of them* – the one Fortune hated
328. *Caius* – Caius may be the name the disguised Kent used when he served Lear.
333. *difference and decay* – quarrels and fall in fortune

LEAR: A plague upon you, murderers, traitors all!
    I might have saved her. Now she's gone for ever!
    Cordelia, Cordelia! Stay a little. Ha!
    What is it thou say'st? Her voice was ever soft,
    Gentle, and low, an excellent thing in woman.
    I killed the slave that was a-hanging thee.
GENTLEMAN: 'Tis true, my lords, he did.
LEAR: Did I not, fellow?
    I have seen the day, with my good biting falchion   320
    I would have made them skip. I am old now,
    And these same crosses spoil me. Who are you?
    Mine eyes are not of the best. I'll tell you straight.
KENT: If Fortune brag of two she loved and hated,
    One of them we behold.
LEAR: This is a dull sight. Are you not Kent?
KENT: The same —
    Your servant Kent. Where is your servant Caius?
LEAR: He's a good fellow, I can tell you that.
    He'll strike, and quickly too. He's dead and rotten.   330
KENT: No, my good lord. I am the very man —
LEAR: I'll see that straight.
KENT: That from your first of difference and decay
    Have followed your sad steps.
LEAR: You are welcome hither.

KENT: Nor no man else! All's cheerless, dark, and deadly.
Your eldest daughters have fordone themselves,
And desperately are dead.

LEAR: Ay, so I think.

ALBANY: He knows not what he says, and vain is it   340
That we present us to him.

EDGAR: Very bootless.

Enter a Messenger.

CAPTAIN: Edmund is dead, my lord.

ALBANY: That's but a trifle here.
You lords and noble friends, know our intent.
What comfort to this great decay may come
Shall be applied. For us, we will resign,
During the life of this old Majesty,
To him our absolute power.

[To Edgar and Kent.]

                    You to your rights,   350
With boot, and such addition as your honours
Have more than merited. All friends shall taste
The wages of their virtue, and all foes
The cup of their deservings. O, see, see!

337. *fordone* – killed

342. *bootless* – useless

346. *great decay* – i.e., Lear

347. *resign* – Albany restores Lear's kingly power. There is a happier ending to Lear's story according to legend: Lear rules for another three years and is succeeded by Cordelia.

351. *boot ... addition* – titles and rights

RELATED READING

The Happy Ending King Lear – drama by Nahum Tate (page 175)

355. *fool* – i.e., Cordelia. Some scholars suggest that this may be a reference to Lear's Fool, who inexplicably disappeared in Act Three, Scene 6.

RELATED READING

A Dog, a Horse, a Rat – poem by A.S. Byatt (page 172)

"After surviving so many sufferings, Lear can only die; and what more truly tragic end for him than to die from grief for the death of Cordelia? And if he is to be saved and to pass the remainder of his days in happiness, the whole loses its signification."
– August Schlegel (1767 – 1845), German poet and scholar

370. *usurped* – suffered longer than anyone should in his circumstances

RELATED READING

Why Lear Must Die – poem by Victor Hugo (page 181)

374. *gored* – wounded
377. *weight* – heavy sorrow
377 – 380. Some scholars argue that this last speech should be delivered by Albany since he is the highest ranking noble to survive. However, the phrase *"We that are young"* sounds as if it should be spoken by Edgar.

LEAR: And my poor fool is hanged! No, no, no life!
　　Why should a dog, a horse, a rat, have life,
　　And thou no breath at all? Thou'lt come no more,
　　Never, never, never, never, never!
　　Pray you undo this button. Thank you, sir.
　　Do you see this? Look on her! Look! Her lips! 　　360
　　Look there, look there!

He dies.

EDGAR: He faints! My lord, my lord!
KENT: Break, heart, I prithee break!
EDGAR: Look up, my lord.
KENT: Vex not his ghost. O, let him pass! He hates him
　　That would upon the rack of this tough world
　　Stretch him out longer.
EDGAR: He is gone indeed.
KENT: The wonder is, he hath endured so long.
　　He but usurped his life. 　　370
ALBANY: Bear them from hence. Our present business
　　Is general woe.
[To Kent and Edgar.] 　　Friends of my soul, you twain
　　Rule in this realm, and the gored state sustain.
KENT: I have a journey, sir, shortly to go.
　　My master calls me; I must not say no.
EDGAR: The weight of this sad time we must obey.
　　Speak what we feel, not what we ought to say.
　　The oldest have borne most. We that are young
　　Shall never see so much, nor live so long. 　　380

Exeunt with a dead march.

FINIS.

ta ta ta

Act Five Considerations

ACT FIVE Scene 1

▶ After reading this scene carefully, choose three major characters and one quotation for each character that you think reveals an essential element of his or her personality or motivation. Explain your choice of quotations in a paragraph.

▶ Supermarket tabloids thrive on hearsay and half-truths. Write a tabloid article based on any detail found in this scene. Express your gossip cautiously to avoid making libellous statements.

▶ Why does Edgar choose to inform Albany of Goneril's letter in the manner that he does? Write a short soliloquy in prose in which Edgar explains his behaviour.

ACT FIVE Scene 2

▶ According to all of Shakespeare's sources for the play, Cordelia's French forces are successful in defeating the armies of Regan and Goneril. Why do you think Shakespeare made Cordelia's army lose?

ACT FIVE Scene 3

▶ Cordelia speaks five lines in this scene and then disappears. Study these lines carefully. How are they different from the rest of the play? Explain why the first two lines of her speech would make a fitting epitaph for her.

▶ Write a short speech for Albany that explains why he stopped the fight before Edgar could kill Edmund.

▶ All the major elements of the plot are resolved in this scene. In groups, develop a prime-time news report covering one of the plot resolutions. Include interviews and news analyses. Group members might take any of these roles: news anchor, reporter, character from the play, or expert commentator.

▶ Read the quotation by G.L. Kittredge on page 138. What do you think he means when he says "amnesia on everybody's part is necessary for the climax that follows"?

▶ Does Lear die joyfully, believing that Cordelia lives? Or is he grief-stricken with the realization that she is dead? Because of the lack of stage directions, it is impossible to answer these questions with certainty. In a short composition, state your opinion and the reasons behind it.

▶ In the Quarto edition of the play, the last speech is given by Albany. In the Folio edition, however, these lines are spoken by Edgar. If you were directing the play, would you assign the speech to Albany or to Edgar? Express your opinion, with reasons, in a persuasive paragraph.

Ten Challenging Questions about *King Lear*

Shakespeare's works have survived for over 400 years. His plays continue to be read, studied, performed, and enjoyed by people all over the world. Shakespeare's legacy is a host of unforgettable characters in great stories, speaking classic lines that contain some of the most powerful poetry ever written.

Perhaps another important reason why Shakespeare continues to fascinate readers and audiences is that his plays can be interpreted in so many different ways. It is ironic that Shakespeare's greatest strength is perhaps his most frustrating quality.

The play *King Lear* poses a number of very interesting and challenging questions. Choose one or more of the following for closer focus and study. The result of your efforts may take the form of a research essay, an independent study project, or a position paper. To address these questions, you will need to probe the text carefully and consult secondary sources. You must also be prepared to choose a position on these issues.

1. The Fool disappears in Act Three, Scene 6, and is not heard from again. Or is he? Some scholars argue that Lear refers to him in Act Five, Scene 3, line 355. What do you think happened to the Fool? In considering your response, examine the role of the Fool in this play.

2. Shakespeare used a variety of sources in writing this play. See Sources of the Play on page 8, and choose one or more of these sources for closer study. How faithful was Shakespeare to the source material? What major differences are there between the source material and Shakespeare's play?

3. Shakespeare's *King Lear* contains two parallel plots: that of Lear and his daughters and that of Gloucester and his sons. The plot of Gloucester and his sons does not appear in any of Shakespeare's sources for *King Lear*. Why then might Shakespeare have included it in his play?

4. To some readers, Lear's treatment of his daughters might be considered unjust. To others, Goneril's and Regan's treatment of their father would be considered cruel. Was Lear "more sinned against than sinning?"

5. Nahum Tate's "The Happy Ending *King Lear*" (see page 175) held the stage for over 150 years. Tate's complete play is available in many libraries. Read Tate's version and compare his treatment of Lear's story with Shakespeare's by analyzing the major differences. Why might some people prefer Tate's version to Shakespeare's?

6. Examine fully the truth and implications of this statement: To understand Cordelia is to understand the whole play. In preparing your response, consider Cordelia's role in the play and how understanding her might shed light on the play itself.

7. According to American scholar Alvin Kernan, *King Lear* "undertakes to defend the justice of the gods in the face of the evidence of overwhelming evil in the world the gods make or control." What different views of the gods are held by the various major characters in this play?

8. Follow the repetition of the word "nothing" throughout the play, examining the contexts in which it is used and its significance.

9. How old is the Fool? Some scholars argue that the Fool is young, which might explain Lear's gentleness toward him. Others maintain that the Fool is older and is one who has gained wisdom with age. Read the Fool's scenes carefully and form your own opinion of the age of the Fool. Explain fully.

10. It is important in the resolution of a tragedy that tragic heroes recognize their weaknesses or flaws. British writer George Orwell describes Lear as "a majestic old man in a long black robe, with flowing white hair and beard, ... wandering through a storm and cursing the heavens.... Presently the scene shifts and the old man, still cursing, still understanding nothing, is holding a dead girl in his arms." Do you agree with Orwell's estimation that the play ends with Lear understanding nothing?

The power of Shakespeare's King Lear *is the subject of the following two sonnets. The first was written by English Romantic poet John Keats (1795–1821) and the second by Margaret Stinson, a Canadian, who wrote this poem when she was a student.*

by John Keats

On SITTING DOWN to READ KING LEAR ONCE AGAIN

O golden tongued Romance, with serene lute!

Fair plumed Syren, Queen of far-away!

Leave melodizing on this wintry day,

Shut up thine olden pages, and be mute:

Adieu! for, once again, the fierce dispute

Betwixt damnation and impassion'd clay

Must I burn through; once more humbly assay

The bitter-sweet of this Shakespearian fruit:

Chief Poet! and ye clouds of Albion,

Begetters of our deep eternal theme!

When through the old oak Forest I am gone,

Let me not wander in a barren dream,

But, when I am consumed in the fire

Give me new Phoenix wings to fly at my desire.

147

by Margaret Stinson

Student Matinee,
STRATFORD

Within the circle, on that sun-warmed hill,

Their faces keen, perceptive, stern in thought,

They sensed old magic, felt their pulses thrill,

Studied the lessons there by Shakespeare taught.

They saw Wrong rampant, rational and bold,

Glimpsed silent Truth, Cordelia's blue and gold,

Heard Lear from depths curse evil in mankind,

And felt no kinship with the tortured mind.

In bright array their freshness rippled round

The patterned apron's geometric score

Whose deepest soundings none has ever found

While youth is new and love forever sure.

But, faith dismayed, or trusted love proven hard,

Time offers wisdom only to the scarred.

Identify the feelings that are expressed in these two sonnets. How do the poets convey these emotions?

Write a sonnet, short poem, or paragraph that expresses how you feel about any aspect of the play *King Lear.*

Caporushes

by Flora Annie Steel

This English fairy tale, retold by novelist Flora Annie Steel (1847–1929), bears a remarkable similarity to the story of King Lear and his daughters.

Once upon a time, a long, long while ago, when all the world was young and all sorts of strange things happened, there lived a very rich gentleman whose wife had died leaving him three lovely daughters. They were as the apple of his eye, and he loved them exceedingly.

Now one day he wanted to find out if they loved him in return, so he said to the eldest, "How much do you love me, my dear?"

And she answered as pat as may be, "As I love my life."

"Very good, my dear," said he, and gave her a kiss. Then he said to the second girl, "How much do you love me, my dear?"

And she answered as swift as thought, "Better than all the world beside."

"Good!" he replied, and patted her on the cheek. Then he turned to the youngest, who was also the prettiest.

"And how much do *you* love me, my dearest?"

Now the youngest daughter was not only pretty, she was clever. So she thought a moment, then she said slowly:

"I love you as fresh meat loves salt!"

Now when her father heard this he was very angry, because he really loved her more than the others.

"What!" he said. "If that is all you give me in return for all I've given you, out of my house you go." So there and then he turned her out of the home where she had been born and bred, and shut the door in her face.

Not knowing where to go, she wandered on, and she wandered on, till she came to a big fen where the reeds grew ever so tall and the rushes swayed in the wind like a field of corn. There she sate down and plaited herself an overall of rushes and a cap to match, so as to hide her fine clothes, and her beautiful golden hair that was all set with milk-white pearls. For she was a wise girl, and thought that in such lonely country, mayhap, some robber might fall in with her and kill her to get her fine clothes and jewels.

It took a long time to plait the dress and cap, and while she plaited she sang a little song:

"Hide my hair, O cap o' rushes,
Hide my heart, O robe o' rushes.
Sure! my answer had no fault,
I love him more than he loves salt."

And the fen birds sate and listened and sang back to her:

"Cap o' rushes, shed no tear,
Robe o' rushes, have no fear;
With these words if fault he'd find,
Sure your father must be blind."

Related Readings

When her task was finished she put on her robe of rushes and it hid all her fine clothes, and she put on the cap and it hid all her beautiful hair, so that she looked quite a common country girl. But the fen birds flew away, singing as they flew:

"Cap-o-rushes! we can see,
Robe o' rushes! what you be,
Fair and clean, and fine and tidy,
So you'll be whate'er betide ye."

By this time she was very, very hungry, so she wandered on, and she wandered on; but ne'er a cottage or a hamlet did she see, till just at sun-setting she came on a great house on the edge of the fen. It had a fine front door to it; but mindful of her dress of rushes she went round to the back. And there she saw a strapping fat scullion washing pots and pans with a very sulky face. So, being a clever girl, she guessed what the maid was wanting, and said:

"If I may have a night's lodging, I will scrub the pots and pans for you."

"Why! Here's luck," replied the scullery-maid, ever so pleased. "I was just wanting badly to go a-walking with my sweetheart. So if you will do my work you shall share my bed and have a bite of my supper. Only mind you scrub the pots clean or cook will be at me."

Now next morning the pots were scraped so clean that they looked like new, and the saucepans were polished like silver, and the cook said to the scullion, "Who cleaned these pots? Not you, I'll swear." So the maid had to up and out with the truth. Then the cook would have turned away the old maid and put on the new, but the latter would not hear of it.

"The maid was kind to me and gave me a night's lodging," she said. "So now I will stay without wage and do the dirty work for her."

So Caporushes—for so they called her since she would give no other name—stayed on and cleaned the pots and scraped the saucepans.

Now it so happened that her master's son came of age, and to celebrate the occasion a ball was given to the neighbourhood, for the young man was a grand dancer, and loved nothing so well as a country measure. It was a very fine party, and after supper was served, the servants were allowed to go and watch the quality from the gallery of the ball-room.

But Caporushes refused to go, for she also was a grand dancer, and she was afraid that when she heard the fiddles starting a merry jig, she might start dancing. So she excused herself by saying she was too tired with scraping pots and washing saucepans; and when the others went off, she crept up to her bed.

But alas! and alack-a-day! The door had been left open, and as she lay in her bed she could hear the fiddlers fiddling away and the tramp of dancing feet.

Then she upped and off with her cap and robe of rushes, and there she was ever so fine and tidy. She was in the ball-room in a trice joining in the jig, and none was more beautiful or better dressed than she. While as for her dancing ... !

Her master's son singled her out at once, and with the finest of bows engaged her as his partner for the rest of the night. So she danced away to her heart's content, while the whole room was agog, trying to find out who the beautiful young stranger could be. But she kept her own counsel and, making some excuse, slipped away before the ball finished; so when her fellow-servants came to bed, there she was in hers in her cap and robe of rushes, pretending to be fast asleep.

Next morning, however, the maids could talk of nothing but the beautiful stranger.

Related Readings

"You should ha' seen her," they said. "She was the loveliest young lady as ever you see, not a bit like the likes o' we. Her golden hair was all silvered wi' pearls, and her dress—law! You wouldn't believe how she was dressed. Young master never took his eyes off her."

And Caporushes only smiled and said, with a twinkle in her eye, "I should like to see her, but I don't think I ever shall."

"Oh yes, you will," they replied, "for young master has ordered another ball tonight in hopes she will come to dance again."

But that evening Caporushes refused once more to go to the gallery, saying she was too tired with cleaning pots and scraping saucepans. And once more when she heard the fiddlers fiddling she said to herself, "I must have one dance—just one with the young master: he dances so beautifully." For she felt certain he would dance with her.

And sure enough, when she had upped and offed with her cap and robe of rushes, there he was at the door waiting for her to come; for he had determined to dance with no one else.

So he took her by the hand, and they danced down the ball-room. It was a sight of all sights! Never were such dancers! So young, so handsome, so fine, so gay!

But once again Caporushes kept her own counsel and just slipped away on some excuse in time, so that when her fellow-servants came to their beds they found her in hers, pretending to be fast asleep; but her cheeks were all flushed and her breath came fast. So they said, "She is dreaming. We hope her dreams are happy."

But next morning they were full of what she had missed. Never was such a beautiful young gentleman as young master! Never was such a beautiful young lady! Never was such beautiful dancing! Every one else had stopped theirs to look on.

And Caporushes, with a twinkle in her eyes, said, "I should like to see her; but I'm *sure* I never shall!"

"Oh yes!" they replied. "If you come tonight you're sure to see her; for young master has ordered another ball in hopes the beautiful stranger will come again; for it's easy to see he is madly in love with her."

Then Caporushes told herself she would not dance again, since it was not fit for a gay young master to be in love with his scullery-maid; but, alas! the moment she heard the fiddlers fiddling, she just upped and offed with her rushes, and there she was fine and tidy as ever! She didn't even have to brush her beautiful golden hair! And once again she was in the ball-room in a trice, dancing away with young master, who never took his eyes off her, and implored her to tell him who she was. But she kept her own counsel and only told him that she never, never, never would come to dance any more, and that he must say good-bye. And he held her hand so fast that she had a job to get away, and lo and behold! his ring came off his finger, and as she ran up to her bed there it was in her hand! She had just time to put on her cap and robe of rushes, when her fellow-servants came trooping in and found her awake.

"It was the noise you made coming upstairs," she made excuse; but they said,

She had just time to put on her cap and robe of rushes, when her fellow-servants came trooping in and found her awake.

"Not we! It is the whole place that is in an uproar searching for the beautiful stranger. Young master he tried to detain her; but she slipped from him like an eel. But he declares he will find her; for if he doesn't he will die of love for her."

Then Caporushes laughed. "Young men don't die of love," says she. "He will find some one else."

But he didn't. He spent his whole time looking for his beautiful dancer, but go where he might, and ask whom he would, he never heard anything about her. And day by day he grew thinner and thinner, and paler and paler, until at last he took to his bed.

And day by day he grew thinner and thinner, and paler and paler, until at last he took to his bed.

And the housekeeper came to the cook and said, "Cook the nicest dinner you can cook, for young master eats nothing."

Then the cook prepared soups, and jellies, and creams, and roast chicken, and bread sauce; but the young man would have none of them.

And Caporushes cleaned the pots and scraped the saucepans and said nothing.

Then the housekeeper came crying and said to the cook, "Prepare some gruel for the young master. Mayhap he'd take that. If not he will die for love of the beautiful dancer. If she could see him now she would have pity on him."

So the cook began to make the gruel, and Caporushes left scraping saucepans and watched her.

"Let me stir it," she said, "while you fetch a cup from the pantry-room."

So Caporushes stirred the gruel, and what did she do but slip young master's ring into it before the cook came back!

Then the butler took the cup upstairs on a silver salver. But when the young master saw it he waved it away, till the butler with tears begged him just to taste it.

So the young master took a silver spoon and stirred the gruel; and he felt something hard at the bottom of the cup. And when he fished it up, lo! it was his own ring! Then he sate up in bed and said quite loud, "Send for the cook!"

And when she came he asked her who made the gruel.

"I did," she said, for she was half-pleased and half-frightened.

Then he looked at her all over and said, "No, you didn't! You're too stout! Tell me who made it and you shan't be harmed!"

Then the cook began to cry. "If you please, sir, I *did* make it; but Caporushes stirred it."

"And who is Caporushes?" asked the young man.

"If you please, sir, Caporushes is the scullion," whimpered the cook.

Then the young man sighed and fell back on his pillow. "Send Caporushes here," he said in a faint voice; for he really was very near dying.

And when Caporushes came he just looked at her cap and her robe of rushes and turned his face to the wall; but he asked her in a weak little voice, "From whom did you get that ring?"

Now when Caporushes saw the poor young man so weak and worn with love for her, her heart melted, and she replied softly:

"From him that gave it me," quoth she, and offed with her cap and robe of rushes, and there she was as fine and tidy as ever with her beautiful golden hair all silvered over with pearls.

And the young man caught sight of her with the tail of his eye, and sate up in bed as strong as may be, and drew her to him and gave her a great big kiss.

So, of course, they were to be married in spite of her being only a scullery-maid, for she told no one who she was. Now every one far and near was asked to the wedding. Amongst the invited guests was Caporushes' father, who, from grief at losing his favourite daughter, had lost his sight, and was very dull and miserable. However, as a friend of the family, he had to come to the young master's wedding.

Now the marriage feast was to be the finest ever seen; but Caporushes went to her friend the cook and said:

"Dress every dish without one mite of salt."

"That'll be rare and nasty," replied the cook; but because she prided herself on having let Caporushes stir the gruel and so saved the young master's life, she did as she was asked, and dressed every dish for the wedding breakfast without one mite of salt.

Now when the company sate down to table their faces were full of smiles and content, for all the dishes looked so nice and tasty; but no sooner had the guests begun to eat than their faces fell; for nothing can be tasty without salt.

Then Caporushes' blind father, whom his daughter had seated next to her, burst out crying.

"What is the matter?" she asked.

Then the old man sobbed, "I had a daughter whom I loved dearly, dearly. And I asked her how much she loved me, and she replied, 'As fresh meat loves salt.' And I was angry with her and turned her out of house and home, for I thought she didn't love me at all. But now I see she loved me best of all."

And as he said the words his eyes were opened, and there beside him was his daughter lovelier than ever.

And she gave him one hand, and her husband, the young master, the other, and laughed saying, "I love you both as fresh meat loves salt." And after that they were all happy for evermore. ∎

> Caporushes went to her friend the cook and said: "Dress every dish without one mite of salt."

In groups of two or more, list the similarities and significant differences between this fairy tale and Shakespeare's *King Lear.*

Research the illustrated fairy tale format used in children's books. Create your own illustrated storybook of this tale or of Shakespeare's *King Lear,* simplifying the plot as necessary. Draw, trace, or use magazine pictures for your illustrations.

KING LEAR IN RESPITE CARE

by Margaret Atwood

Canadian poet, short story writer, and novelist Margaret Atwood
(b. 1939) illustrates how, in the words of Goethe (1749–1832),
"an aged man is always a King Lear."

The daughters have their parties.
Who can cope?
He's left here in a chair
he can't get out of
in all this snow, or possibly
wallpaper. Wheeled somewhere.
He will have to be sly and stubborn
and not let on.

Another man's hand
coming out of a tweed sleeve that isn't
his, curls on his knee. He can move it with the other
hand. Howling would be uncalled for.

Who knows what he knows?
Many things, but where he is
isn't among them. How did it happen,
this cave, this hovel?
It may or may not be noon.

Time is another element
you never think about
until it's gone.
Things like ceilings, or air.

Someone comes to brush
his hair, wheel him to tea-time.
Old women gather around
in pearls and florals. They want to flirt.
An old man is so rare.
He's a hero just by being here.

They giggle. They disappear
behind the hawthorn bushes
in bloom, or possibly sofas.
Now he's been left alone
with the television turned on
to the weather program, the sound down.

The cold blast sweeps across
the waste field of the afternoon.
Rage occurs,
followed by supper:
something he can't taste,
a brownish texture.

The sun goes down. The trees bend,
they straighten up. They bend.
At eight the youngest daughter comes.
She holds his hand.
She says, *Did they feed you?*
He says no.
He says, *Get me out of here.*
He wants so much to say *please*,
but won't.

After a pause, she says—
he hears her say—
I love you like salt.

According to this poem, what conditions are experienced by senior citizens in respite care? Use details from the poem to support your conclusions.

Who do you think is the speaker in this poem? What might be the purpose for writing it? Explore your thoughts by writing a short poem or paragraph, from the point of view of the speaker, in which the speaker's identity and motivation for writing the poem are revealed.

Nothing Shall Come of Nothing

by Mairi MacInnes

Just as Shakespeare retold older tales, many modern works retell Shakespeare's stories using contemporary settings. The following selection is from American author Mairi MacInnes's novel The Quondam Wives *(1993). It parallels the opening action of* King Lear.

Anthony Quondam hurried along the gravel path from the garden front of his big old house to the stable block with the slightly hectic, slightly effeminate trot of an old man. His shanks had lost some muscle and his pelvis had broadened. His spine had lost its arch and begun to curve forward, a tendency he fought by habitually throwing his chest out. He carried his large silvery head askew to balance a shoulder that was now carried lower than the other one. His bright dark eyes stared out enthusiastically from under his black hairy brows and the wild mane of white hair that he kept stroking back with one hand. He had decided to let his beard grow, and it was coming out as white as the hair on his head but bushier, and he was not sure whether to keep it or shave it off. He would ask Delia whether she liked it.

He liked Delia. She continually astonished him as his other daughters failed to do. He thought often how beautiful and talented she was, and how she was yet his daughter. Alone he had begot her, bred her, loved her. Now he was going to reward inscrutable fate by giving her the best part of his house. He couldn't wait to tell her. He knew he would find her in the studio he had set up for her after she'd gone down from university. The barn she inhabited opened off the old kennel yard and was oak and stone, solid, with a good dry floor. In its airy sweet-smelling space, Anthony had installed an immense cast-iron stove that had once warmed the waiting room of York Station. He had also double-glazed the slits that provided air and light and put in skylights of Perspex on the northern side. There was a double door to keep out the cold and wet. The space was now quiet and warm, and its light was a pure Arctic light, devoid of yellow, that brought out detail without casting much shadow. As he entered it, Delia appeared in startling focus wearing a plain white shirt and dark cotton trousers in the heart of a black and white photograph. She had put her current canvases face to the wall and was simply standing, contemplating, pencil or pen or charcoal stick in hand, before an easel to which she had pinned a large sheet of paper. There was a large elaborate drawing on it, apparently of figures in a landscape. He closed the door and stood before her, panting. If the other dear girls had spoken of their love for him in a fine exaggerated way, shouldn't Delia outdo them, since he loved her fifty times more than he loved them?

"Delia, I had to see you."

She came forward smiling and pulled a kitchen chair from a wreckage of canvases and frames in a corner.

"You need a comfortable chair in here," he said. "Or two chairs. Why don't you ask for them?"

157

"I'm all right!"

"Of course you're 'all right,' but it's not very comfortable for you, darling. I want you to have everything you feel you need."

"It's perfectly comfortable, Dad"—and waited, still with a slight, delighted smile.

"That's so wonderful!"—jerking his head at the drawing. She immediately picked a white cloth off the back of the easel and covered the paper. "Sorry, I shouldn't ... "

"It's just that ... "

"Don't explain. You like to keep it unseen until you've finished it." She nodded, not an inch more than was necessary.

"All your work, it seems to me, is *wonderful.*"

She shook her head and went red. At the same time her eyes unexpectedly welled with tears.

He was astounded. "Ah, Delia! What have I said to disturb you? And I had such good things to tell you!" He was terribly upset at her tears. They fell in silence, running down her cheeks and wetting her white shirt with long smears, and she made no move to mop them or stop them. "What's wrong, can't I praise your work?"

"No." Her voice was perfectly clear.

"Don't you love me, Delia, my darling child?"

"Of course."

"Can't a father delight in his daughter's work?"

"I haven't done anything delightful. Your delight has nothing to do with me." She threw the cloth back, ripped the paper off the easel and tore it in half and those halves again in half and threw the shreds on the floor. Then she dried her eyes with the handkerchief he offered her and stood staring at him, clearly wishing him to go. "What have you come to see me about?"

But the rapture of his generosity had passed and he felt an outsider on his own property, humiliated by a girl sixty years younger than he was, flesh of his flesh, blood of his blood, who wished him dead. Nevertheless he went on with what he had to say. He could not just turn and go. He could not find a more congenial moment to speak than this one. Even now, when she heard what he had to say, she might relent, she might throw her arms round his neck. It was not impossible. She had often thrown her arms round his neck when she was a little child. A more adorable child it was hard to imagine. Now, a grown woman, she might come to the point of apologising. Apology cost nothing. It was a gesture, nothing more. She could surely afford a little gesture towards her father. His voice became unnaturally syrupy. "I came to tell you that your mother and I are leaving the hall and going to live in Akeld as soon as it can be fixed up. We're splitting the hall and the estate into three parts, one for you, one for Gwen, one for Reggie."

He waited. He even thought she might cry again, this time out of love and gratitude. If she did, he would embrace her wholeheartedly, understanding that she had to balance her mysterious resentment with a clear and candid receptivity. He said to her fondly, "Nothing is guaranteed to us, Delia." He meant to imply that fate is paramount.

She said, "I don't want any part of it."

"Alice ran away, with your sisters, to survive, I honestly believe. But you know, Delia, I found them boring, your sisters. So narrow, so pious in some piety I didn't recognise. Do you know what I'm saying, darling? I haven't threatened you, have I? You know what: a tree, to flourish, must have its roots in the mud. My roots are in the mud, I think. Oh, I am sorry to be so old. So difficult for you. I had a past, Delia. You can't have dreamed of it. It's of no consequence to you now, I understand that clearly. I don't prize it myself. But it is there, if you have need of it. If you ever have to take me seriously." She fidgeted and said nothing, and kept her eyes on the floor in front of her. After a moment, he heard himself pleading. "I thought you'd be glad of my present. Why are you behaving in this churlish fashion? I'll give you the state-rooms and the stable block, with the rose garden and the orchard and the dovecot. You'll be independent. You'll have a special fund put aside specially to convert it into your very own house, exactly the way you want it."

"But I don't want it." She spoke in a low, clear voice as if she had been rehearsing with a master. "Believe me, you're very kind, but I'm happy as I am. Thank you. Don't think I don't love you. I honour you in everything you do."

Anthony stared at her bitterly. "So, thank you very much. You can't stay here, you know, after we've gone. We're giving the place to your sisters too, so if you don't want your part of the hall and the stable block, you can leave."

"If you want me to leave, I shall do so. I won't stay with Reggie and Gwen. I know them."

"You can go and live in a damned caravan in a caravan park and see how you like that," he shouted.

"If you wish it."

"And don't think you'll get a pretty cottage or anything like that, because there aren't any. I've sold as many as I couldn't rent and I can't afford to do more." The blood gathered behind his eyes, squeezing them forward, and a sliver of pain crept along a crevice in his forehead just above his left eye.

"I don't want you to do more." Her voice became soft, as if she were tired. Even Gwen and Reggie had more bounce in their voices when he telephoned them, and of course they had said, each in her way, that they were immensely fond of him. He couldn't think what had got into this one, whom he'd been mistaken in believing the best of the lot.

"The sooner you go the better, then. We're moving to Akeld. Did you think perhaps you were getting Akeld? It was you who told me the Amorys were leaving. So we're having it done up." He staggered to his feet, kicking over the kitchen chair. "Not a kiss? Nothing? To hell with you then." He got to the door somehow.

"Wait," said Delia.

He stood shaking at the door. "Yes?"

She spoke painfully. "You're giving away everything? For nothing?"

"*What?*"

"Giving it away for nothing?"

"For nothing. For love." The phrase pleased him.

"But it's yours. You can't give it away."

"What rubbish! I can give it away exactly because it's mine."

Her painfulness increased. "Even if you gave it away, it would still be yours. That's how I see it. I can't take what is yours."

"Nothing shall come of nothing!"

"Let *them* say what you want to hear."

"They will! They do!" He waited another second before flinging open the door and rushing out, but she showed no expression.

To what extent are the characters and events in this story similar to those in Shakespeare's play? How are they different?

Why do authors sometimes use other people's plots and characters in their works? Write a composition in which you explore your thoughts and feelings on this issue.

WISE ENOUGH to PLAY the FOOL

by Isaac Asimov

American scientist and writer Isaac Asimov (1920–1992) is perhaps best known for his classic science fiction works. An author of over one hundred books, he also wrote on many other subjects. In the following selection, taken from his two-volume study of Shakespeare, Asimov reveals the secret of the successful fool.

In Shakespearean London, and for a considerable length of time afterward, it was considered fun to visit Bethlehem Hospital and watch the madmen....

If a madman were sufficiently harmless and amusing—if, for instance, he could make "witless" remarks that were nevertheless humorous—he might be kept for the purpose by a family that was sufficiently well off to afford to feed a useless mouth. Naturally, a shrewd but poor fellow could see that if he but pretended to be slightly mad and took care to be pungently clever, he might get a good job.

The court fool became a standard part of the palace scene, then, and was the analogue of the modern television set, for ideally, he could do comic songs and dances, make witty comments, do sight gags, and so on. It was anachronistic to introduce one into pre-Roman Britain, but the audience would

scarcely worry about that. In Shakespeare's time the court fool still flourished, though they were to vanish from the scene within a generation of his death.

Naturally, such a fool could say and do things an ordinary man could not possibly get away with. Behind the protection of his own madness and the amusement of his royal patron, he could mock arrogant lords and stately bishops and cast aspersions on all the sacred cows.

Any fool (not as mad as he seemed, usually, and someone who might well be the most intelligent member of the court) would find it hard to resist puncturing the emptiest heads, and if those heads lacked a sense of humor (as they naturally would), the fool would make himself extremely unpopular....

Licensed fools had standardized costumes, of which one noticeable item was the hat, which had sewn to it a piece of serrated red cloth to represent a cockscomb. The cock, after all, is a stupid creature filled with a foolish pride and given to making senseless sounds, so that there seems a resemblance between cock and fool.

The hat is, therefore, a "cockscomb," or, as universally spelled, a coxcomb. The term has come to be shifted from the appurtenance of a fool to the fool himself. A stupid man, particularly one who is vain and arrogant, is a coxcomb....

The special costume of a court fool serves two purposes. First, it is a silly costume which is designed to stir laughter in itself and make the task of the fool easier. Second, it advertises his function and makes it plain to anyone within sight that he is a privileged character.

Naturally, a costume intended to catch the eye at once must be conspicuous. In addition to the coxcomb, therefore, the Fool wears a costume of rough varicolored wool, so that he is a mélange of patched colors. This is called "motley," and the word itself is the badge of the fool.

The Fool uses the word in a little verse he improvises as part of his grim remarks on the folly of Lear's division of the kingdom. (It is virtually his one subject—a mournful bell tolling a single note.)

He points out there are sweet (amusing) fools and bitter (stupid) fools. Pointing first to himself and then to Lear, he says:

The sweet and bitter fool
    Will presently appear;
The one in motley here,
    The other found out there.
                    (1.4.134–137)

Lear, frowning, demands to know if he is being called a fool. The Fool replies caustically:

All thy other titles thou hast given away,
that thou wast born with.
                    (1.4.139–140)

And Kent says, ruefully:

This is not altogether fool, my lord.
                    (1.4.141)

That, of course, is the great secret of the successful fool—that he is no fool at all. ■

Today, the role of the licensed fool is played by the professional comedian and political satirist. Write a composition in which you explore the similarities between the court fool and a current popular comedian or political satirist.

To be successful, the jester had to be "wise enough to play the fool." This paradox has been expressed in various ways. Using a CD-ROM, the Internet, or a book of quotations, find and present to your class at least three pertinent quotations that deal with the paradoxical nature of the fool.

SEND *in* the CLOWNS

by Goenawan Mohamad

Laughter serves an important purpose— especially in tragedy. In the following selection, Indonesian essayist Goenawan Mohamad explores the role of the Fool in King Lear. *Shakespeare is careful when he sends in the clowns. He also knows when it is time for the Fool to exit.*

The Fool has a special, albeit small, role in *King Lear*. To be sure, one should not stretch the meaning of such a minor character too far. Ultimately, the Fool is just Shakespeare's version of a traditional clown. Still, I would suggest that the Fool's role is to be perceived in his relation to power and madness.

He comes into the scene as a part of the monarch's paraphernalia (Lear calls him "my Fool"), but soon he projects himself as somebody who looks with a half-disguised disdain at the members of Lear's court. As he sees it, the kingdom is in upheaval, and all the grandees, including the monarch, are rapidly losing their moral and intellectual force.... By flashing his folk-wisdom and deprecating remarks about the King and his courtiers from time to time, he seems to insinuate that he has the least contaminated view, thanks to his peculiar position, his shrewd common sense, and his plebeian pragmatism. He upbraids the King openly when Lear is beginning to feel the frustration of being a royal emeritus with no political power: "I am better than thou art now. I am Fool, thou art nothing."

From the outset, the Fool is both insider and outsider. He does his job, by attending and entertaining his sovereign, but he consistently rejects being treated as a genuine half-wit. His buffoonery is only an act, he seems to say, and who is the fool, anyway? He or Lear? Or both, "The one in motley here" and "the other found out there"? Or the Earl of Kent? The answer, as he suggests it, is equivocal. For this reason, he detaches himself both from Lear's legitimacy as a king ... and his madness.

The Fool is not unlike Sancho Panza in the imagination of Cervantes. But this fool of Lear's will never swap dreams with his master as Sancho Panza eventually does with Don Quixote. True, Lear's Fool follows the beggarly king into the night and onto the heath, expecting nothing in return, knowing for sure that he goes in harm's way in the loser's camp. But never is his mind servile. He is, indeed, as Lear puts it, "a bitter Fool," sarcastic, contemptuous, no flattering flunkey. Goneril, angered at

her father's unruly retinue, calls him "all-licensed Fool."

In short, he is not another Kent. He has a certain sense of irony that Kent never has. Many will be touched by the Earl of Kent's love and selfless devotion to his King, but not the Fool. He looks at it with a sneer. When Kent, in disguise, unnecessarily roughs up Goneril's man, to display his eagerness to serve the abdicating monarch, the Fool tells him to wear a coxcomb, the professional fool's cap. It is foolish, he tells Kent, to take "one's part that's out of favour." And when at Gloucester's castle he sees the Earl sitting miserably with his legs in the stocks, the Fool laughs. Again he calls Kent a "fool" and again he minds the true-blue gentleman of the old king's declining power and the immediate political repercussions confronting all of Lear's loyalists. "Let go thy hold when a great wheel run down a hill lest it break thy neck with following," he says.

Such a caveat is by no means a Machiavellian opportunist's advice. It speaks not so much of the Fool's preference as of his (or Shakespeare's) way to present a more sober look at things. It is probably his method to counterpoise Kent's zealous sense of loyalty. It is also his way to show his scorn towards the corrupted court. However, whether the Fool has a higher moral stature than the rest is not entirely clear. He suggests that he is different from the knave who "serves and seeks for gain" and he certainly is. But "a bitter fool" as he is, he often exhibits a malicious bent and a crude cynicism that tends to corrode any belief in the possibility of being good. Deprived of the ease and security which he acquired through long years of servitude, he mingles his wisecracks with a precarious faith. "O, Nuncle, court holy-water in a dry-house is better than this rain water out o'door," he says, soaked and wet and cold under the stormy sky.

As things work out, it doesn't take long for the audience to see that before the tragedy reaches its climax, the Fool is no longer with Lear. In the sixth scene, Kent starts to move the old king away to Dover, after learning from Gloucester that there is "a plot of death upon him." The Fool helps Kent to carry Lear, who is asleep, to the litter, and since there is no more word about him, the play omits the Fool, abruptly, persuading a critic to speculate that the reason is Shakespeare's "carelessness or an impatient desire to reduce his overloaded material" (A.C. Bradley, *Shakespearean Tragedy*). But no matter what Shakespeare's reason was when he wrote the continuing parts, somehow the Fool's nonpresence does not create a disconcerting blank in the play.

Along these lines, it is possible to interpret the Fool's disappearance as a point of a new setting: steadily, the play moves into its tragic denouement, allowing no more

... steadily, the play moves into its tragic denouement, allowing no more room for comic diversion....

room for comic diversion.... In a sense, his omission is like the sound of silence before a more frightening time, when humorous laughter is an oddity or even a subversion, when common sense, a prudent approach to things, detachment from great ambitions, no longer work. It is a time of an entirely different madness—the madness of the powerful, not the madness of the victim. At this stage, Goneril and Regan and Edmund move to a darker, deeper route in their "tyrannous night," adding cruelty to treason and greed. At this stage, life needs no Fool.

The Fool, after all, is not a figure fit for the act. His essential role is to insert laughter into the play's tragic order, and, as a result, create a certain sense of distance and put Lear's weight of agony into a wider perspective....

So there are moments when the Fool has to go, or to rest. Things like Gloucester's torture, Cordelia's death, Lear's asking for forgiveness, can never be objects of ridicule, if we want to remain human. ■

According to Mohamad, what purposes does the Fool serve in the play? How does the author explain the Fool's disappearance in Act Three?

Once the Fool announces that he "will go to sleep at noon," Shakespeare provides no indication of the Fool's fate. Imagine you were there and saw what happened to the Fool. Write a brief account of the events after the Fool's disappearance in Act Three.

Related Readings

by Mary Jo Salter

Refrain

A refrain is a line or group of lines that is repeated in a poem or song for a variety of effects. American poet Mary Jo Salter illustrates how powerful repetition can be.

> *But let his disposition have that scope*
> *As dotage gives it.*
>
> —Goneril to Albany

Never afflict yourself to know the cause,
said Goneril, her mind already set.
No one can tell us who her mother was

or, knowing, could account then by the laws
of nurture for so false and hard a heart.
Never afflict yourself to know the cause

of Lear's undoing: if without a pause
he shunned Cordelia, as soon he saw the fault.
No one can tell us who her mother was,

but here's a pretty reason seven stars
are seven stars: because they are not eight.
Never afflict yourself to know the cause—

like servants, even one's superfluous.
The king makes a good fool: the Fool is right.
No one can tell him who his mother was

when woman's water-drops are all he has
against the storm, and daughters cast him out.
Never afflict yourself to know the cause;
no one can tell you who your mother was.

What effect is created through the repetition of the phrase "never afflict yourself to know the cause"?

In a short paragraph, explore why you think the author changed the personal pronouns in the last line of the poem.

Write your own "Refrain" poem, choosing a line from the play that you think is especially evocative to repeat. Imitate the structure of Salter's poem if you wish.

Goneril

by Karel Čapek

Czechoslovakian author Karel Čapek (1890–1938) is best known for his science fiction play R.U.R. He also wrote a number of short stories, some of which deal with Shakespearean themes and characters. In the following story, Čapek offers a new perspective on Goneril.

No, nothing's the matter with me, nurse—and don't call me your little pretty one. I know you called me that when I was little; and King Lear called me a young rapscallion, didn't he? He would rather have had a son. Do you think boys are really nicer than girls? Regan was always so ladylike, and Cordelia—you know—so absent-minded. A regular butterfingers. And Regan—there was no saying a word to her: nose in the air like a queen, but selfish, do you remember? She always had it in her. Tell me, nurse, was I bad when I was little? There, you see!

How does one begin to turn wicked? I *know* I'm wicked, nurse. Don't say I'm not; you think so too. I don't mind what you all think of me. Even if you think me wicked. But over that business with father I was in the right, nurse. Why on earth did he get the idea that he must take those hundred fellows of his about with him? and if there had only been a hundred of them, but there were all sorts of rag, tag and bobtail besides—it simply wouldn't do. I'd have liked to have him, nurse, truly I would; I was fond of him, terribly fond, fonder than of anyone else in the world; but those followers of his, my God!—They simply made a bear-garden of the place! Just remember, nurse, what it looked like: full of loafers, nothing but brawls and quarrelling and shouting, and the dirt, well—— Worse than a dunghill. Tell me, nurse, would any mistress of a household have put up with *that?* And *I* couldn't give them orders—oh no! Only King Lear was allowed to order them about. They just made faces at me.

At night they went after the maids—I kept on hearing tapping and rustling and whistling—the duke slept like a log; I used to wake him and say, can't you hear? And he just grunted, leave them alone, and went off to sleep again. Just think what it was like for *me*, nurse, while that was going on! You have been young yourself, you can understand. When I complained to King Lear he just laughed at me: Why, my girl, what else can you expect of the fellows? Stop up your ears and don't think about it.

And so I told him that it wouldn't do, that he must send away at least half of the lazy fellows who were eating me out of house and home. And as you know, he was insulted. He called it ingratitude and I don't know what besides. You've no idea what a rage he flew into. And yet I know what can be done and what can't. Men only bother about their honour, but we women have to think about running the house in an orderly way. *They*

Related Readings

don't care if it's an absolute pigstye. Tell me, nurse, was I right or not? There, you see! And father took it as a deadly insult. What was I to do? I know my duty to him, but as a woman I have a duty to my home, haven't I? And so father cursed me. And the duke—he just stood there, blinking and shifting from one foot to the other. D'you think he stood up for me? No. He let me be treated like a wicked, mean, scolding woman. Listen, nurse, at that moment something seemed to snap inside me: I—I—I began to *hate* my husband. I hate him. There, now you know! *I hate him!* And I hate my father because it's his fault, do you understand? So there you are; I'm wicked, I know, but I'm only wicked because I was in the right——

No, don't say anything; I am really wicked. You know I have a lover, don't you? If you only realized how little I mind your knowing! Do you think I love Edmund? I don't; but I want to be revenged on the duke because he didn't behave like a man. I simply hate him. Nurse, you can't imagine what it is to hate! It means to be bad, bad, bad through and through! When one begins to hate—one seems to change altogether. I used to be quite a good girl, nurse, and I might have grown into a good woman; I used to be a daughter, I used to be a sister, and now I am only wicked. Now I don't love even you, nurse, I don't love even myself—I was in the right; if they had admitted that, I should be a different woman, believe me——

No, I'm not crying. Don't think it makes me sad. Not a bit. One is freer when one hates. One can think what one likes—one

needn't stop at anything. You know, *before* I hadn't the courage to see my husband as he is, to see that he is disagreeable and fat and a coward and that his hands are damp; and now I see it. Now I see that my father Lear is a ridiculous tyrant, that he's a toothless and muddle-headed old man—I see everything. I see that Regan is a viper and that I—Oh, nurse, I have such strange and terrible things in me—I used not to have any idea of it before. It happened all of a sudden. Tell me, is it *my* fault? I was in the right; they shouldn't have driven me so far....

You can't understand it, nurse. Sometimes I feel as if I could kill the duke when he's snoring beside me. Just stick a sword into him. Or poison Regan. Here's a cup of wine for you, sister, drink it up. Did you know that Regan is trying to get Edmund away from me? Not because she loves him; Regan's as cold as a stone. She's just doing it to spite me. And she counts on Edmund clearing that blockhead of a duke out of his way somehow and seizing the throne after Lear's death. I know that's how it is, nurse. Regan's a widow now—she always had luck, the cat. But you needn't think she'll be successful: I'm on the watch and I hate them all. I don't even sleep, I just lie awake thinking and hating. If you only knew how beautifully and boundlessly one can hate in the darkness. And when I remember that it all came about just through father's obstinacy and the mess they made in the house. You must admit no lady could have put up with it....

Nurse, nurse, nurse, why didn't they see all that time ago that I was in the right?

Before you read this story how did you feel about Goneril? To what extent has reading this story changed your first impressions of her? Explain.

By looking at the situation through Goneril's eyes, the author makes her a more believable and sympathetic character. Choose another "wicked" character from the play and write a story similar to Capek's. Aim to enable the reader to sympathize with and better understand the character you have chosen.

Related Readings

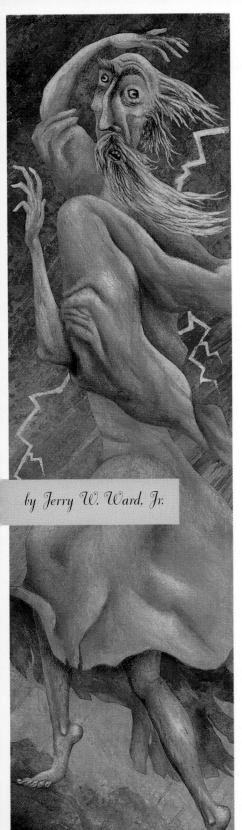

I Dream of Lear

*In his dream of Lear, American poet Jerry W. Ward, Jr.
(b. 1943) emphasizes the power of Shakespeare.
Despite the span of time, we are still able to relate to
Shakespeare's characters and their passions.*

by Jerry W. Ward, Jr.

I dream of Lear,
cracked shadow of a man
unbelted, unbuttoned,
wary of lendings,
shot with storm,
burnt in love's quick thunder.

I dream of him
houseless in his hour
of terrible need.
Rank seeds displace his reason.
Reeking of mortality,
he wanders the rims of spirit worlds.

I dream of him
as politics afflict his soul.
His brain's become a pincushion
of inwit, a ripe carnival of decay.
The bitter rain
lashes him to earth.

Sudden awakening's the blind end
of this game. Assuming his bones,
my body goes tame; my breath comes in spurts.
Glued against my sweating sheets,
unaccommodated, I suffer
the extreme unction of aloneness.

In the last verse of this poem, it is clear that the speaker identifies with Lear. What is
it about Lear that he identifies with? What do you think is meant by the last three
lines of the poem?

Choose a character other than Lear and write a poem similar to Ward's. In the first
three verses, focus on details from the play. In the last verse, focus on some aspect
of that character that you identify with.

THE BLIND LEADING THE BLIND

by *Lisel Mueller*

*In the following poem, American poet Lisel Mueller
(b. 1924) echoes one of the play's recurring themes.*

Take my hand. There are two of us in this cave.
The sound you hear is water; you will hear it forever.
The ground you walk on is rock. I have been here before.
People come here to be born, to discover, to kiss,
to dream and to dig and to kill. Watch for the mud.
Summer blows in with scent of horses and roses;
fall with the sound of sound breaking; winter shoves
its empty sleeve down the dark of your throat.
You will learn toads from diamonds, the fist from the palm,
love from the sweat of love, falling from flying.
There are a thousand turnoffs. I have been here before.
Once I fell off a precipice. Once I found gold.
Once I stumbled on murder, the thin parts of a girl.
Walk on, keep walking, there are axes above us.
Watch for occasional bits and bubbles of light—
birthdays for you, recognitions: *yourself, another.*
Watch for the mud. Listen for bells, for beggars.
Something with wings went crazy against my chest once.
There are two of us here. Touch me.

In what ways is the speaker of this poem similar to Edgar as he leads his father
to Dover?

What ideas about life does Mueller develop in this poem?

Related Readings

by A.S. Byatt

A Dog,
a Horse,
a Rat

*English novelist and literary critic A.S. Byatt (b. 1936)
mourns the passing of a loved one in this eloquent elegy
inspired by Lear's lament over Cordelia's death.*

*Why should a dog, a horse, a rat, have life,
And thou no breath at all?*

A dog, a horse, a rat
All those red-troubled days
Heraldic in my head
Danced in their lively ways.
The bright-eyed rat, so sleek,
The dog with plume and claw
The horse's hot bright neck
And thou wilt come no more
The terror of their life
Their moving flesh, their air
In nostril, lung and heart
He cried, look there, look there,

Fooled by a flutter, Lear—
But I heard what they said
As they remade my life
With their plain "he is dead".

None of my breaths since then
Is easy or is sure
Nothing I think or hear
Without, thou'lt come no more,

A dog, a horse, a rat
I see in bliss and fear
Live fur and bone delight
Wet eye and curling ear

But every breath I draw
In pleasure or in pain
Sings in my flesh and blood
He will not come again

And still, when I live most
And walk in the warm air
My nostrils breathe the ghost
Of your warm yellow hair

My skull contains the lost
Breath of your yellow hair
Of your burned yellow hair.

Explain the significance of the poem's title.

In what ways does the speaker in the poem identify with Lear? What do Lear and the
speaker have in common?

Related Readings

The
HAPPY ENDING
KING LEAR

by Nahum Tate

English dramatist Nahum Tate (1652–1715) was so dissatisfied with the tragic ending of King Lear *that he reinstated the happy conclusion of earlier versions of the story. Tate's version held the stage for over 150 years.*

Scene, a Prison.

Lear asleep, with his head on Cordelia's lap.

CORDELIA: What toils, thou wretched king, hast thou endured
To make thee draw, in chains, a sleep so sound?
Thy better angel charm thy ravished mind
With fancied freedom. Peace is used to lodge
On cottage straw. Thou hast the beggar's bed,
Therefore shouldst have the beggar's careless thought.
And now, my Edgar, I remember thee.
What fate has seized thee in this general wreck
I know not, but I know thou must be wretched
Because Cordelia holds thee dear.   10
O Gods! A sudden gloom overwhelms me, and the image
Of death overspreads the place. Ha! Who are these?

Enter Captain and Officers with cords.

2. *draw* – enjoy

6. *careless* – carefree

15 – 18. Lear awakes in the middle of a dream and thinks that he is still at battle.

23 – 24. *no ... preferment* – It is futile to bribe us with money or position.

29. *dispatch* – kill

Stage Direction: *partisan* – a long-handled spear with a broad head.

34. *impious* – unholy

44. *falchion* – short sword

CAPTAIN: Now, sirs, dispatch, already you are paid
　　In part, the best of your reward is to come.
LEAR: Charge, charge upon their flank, their last wing halts;
　　Push, push the battle, and the day's our own.
　　Their ranks are broke, down, down with Albany.
　　Who holds my hands? O, thou deceiving sleep,
　　I was this very minute on the chase.
　　And now a prisoner here. What mean the slaves?　　　20
　　You will not murder me?
CORDELIA: 　　　　　　　　Help earth and heaven!
　　For your souls' sakes, dear sirs, and for the gods'.
OFFICER: No tears, good lady, no pleading against gold and
　　preferment. Come, sirs, make ready your cords.
CORDELIA: You, sir, I'll seize,
　　You have a human form, and if no prayers
　　Can touch your soul to spare a poor king's life,
　　If there be anything that you hold dear,
　　By that I beg you to dispatch me first.
CAPTAIN: Comply with her request, dispatch her first.　　　30
LEAR: Off, hell-hounds, by the gods I charge you spare her!
　　'Tis my Cordelia, my true pious daughter.
　　No pity? Nay then, take an old man's vengeance.

Snatches a partisan, and strikes down two of them.
The rest quit Cordelia, and turn upon him.
Enter Edgar and Albany with Attendants.

EDGAR: Death! Hell! Ye vultures, hold your impious hands,
　　Or take a speedier death than you would give.
CAPTAIN: By whose command?
EDGAR: 　　　　　　　　Behold the duke, your lord.
ALBANY: Guards, seize those instruments of cruelty.
CORDELIA: My Edgar, oh!
EDGAR: My dear Cordelia! Lucky was the minute
　　Of our approach. The gods have weighed our sufferings;　40
　　We are past the fire, and now must shine to ages.
GENTLEMAN: Look here, my lord, see where the generous King
　　Has slain two of them.
LEAR: 　　　　　　　　Did I not, fellow?
　　I've seen the day, with my good biting falchion.
　　I could have made 'em skip. I am old now,

And these vile crosses spoil me. Out of breath!
Fie, oh! Quite out of breath and spent.
ALBANY: Bring in old Kent; and, Edgar, guide you hither
Your father, whom you said was near.

Exit Edgar.

He may be an ear-witness at the least   50
Of our proceedings.

Kent brought in here.

LEAR: Who are you?
My eyes are none of the best, I'll tell you straight.
Oh, Albany! Well, sir, we are your captives,
And you are come to see death pass upon us.
Why this delay? Or is it your Highness' pleasure
To give us first the torture? Say ye so?
Why here's old Kent and I, as tough a pair
As ever bore tyrant's stroke. But my Cordelia,
My poor Cordelia here, oh pity!
ALBANY: Take off their chains. Thou injured majesty,   60
The wheel of Fortune now has made her circle,
And blessings yet stand 'twixt thy grave and thee.
LEAR: Com'st thou, inhuman lord, to soothe us back
To a fool's paradise of hope, to make
Our doom more wretched? Go to, we are too well
Acquainted with misfortune to be gulled
With lying hope. No, we will hope no more.
ALBANY: I have a tale to unfold so full of wonder
As cannot meet an easy faith.
But by that royal injured head 'tis true.   70
KENT: What would Your Highness?
ALBANY: Know, the noble Edgar
Impeached Lord Edmund since the fight, of treason,
And dared him for the proof to single combat,
In which the gods confirmed his charge by conquest.
I left even now the traitor wounded mortally.
LEAR: And whither tends this story?
ALBANY: Ere they fought
Lord Edgar gave into my hands this paper,
A blacker scroll of treason, and of lust,

53. Lear believes that Albany
is still his enemy since
Albany led the troops against
Cordelia and the French
forces.

66. *gulled* – deceived

Related Readings

Than can be found in the records of hell.
There, sacred sir, behold the character   80
Of Goneril, the worst of daughters, but
More vicious wife.

CORDELIA: Could there be yet addition to their guilt?
What will not they that wrong a father do?

ALBANY: Since then my injuries, Lear, fall in with thine,
I have resolved the same redress for both.

KENT: What says my lord?

CORDELIA: Speak, for methought I heard
The charming voice of a descending god.

ALBANY: The troops by Edmund raised, I have disbanded.
Those that remain are under my command.   90
What comfort may be brought to cheer your age
And heal your savage wrongs, shall be applied;
For to your majesty we do resign
Your kingdom, save what part yourself conferred
On us in marriage.

KENT: Hear you that, my liege?

CORDELIA: Then there are gods, and virtue is their care.

LEAR: Is it possible?
Let the spheres stop their course, the sun make halt,
The winds be hushed, the seas and fountains rest;
All nature pause, and listen to the change.   100
Where is my Kent, my Caius?

KENT: Here, my liege.

LEAR: Why I have news that will recall thy youth.
Ha! Didst thou hear it, or did the inspiring gods
Whisper to me alone? Old Lear shall be
A king again.

KENT: The prince, that like a god has power, has said it.

LEAR: Cordelia then shall be a queen, mark that.
Cordelia shall be queen. Winds, catch the sound
And bear it on your rosy wings to heaven.
Cordelia is a queen.   110

Reenter Edgar with Gloster.

85. *fall in with* – resemble
86. *redress* – remedy. Albany has decided to relinquish his position.

ALBANY: Look, sir, where pious Edgar comes
    Leading his eyeless father. O my liege!
    His wondrous story will deserve your leisure.
    What he has done and suffered for your sake,
    What for the fair Cordelia's.

GLOSTER: Where is my liege? Conduct me to his knees to hail
    His second birth of empire. My dear Edgar
    Has, with himself, revealed the king's blest restoration.

LEAR: My poor dark Gloster.

GLOSTER: O let me kiss that once more sceptered hand!   120

LEAR: Hold, thou mistak'st the majesty, kneel here.
    Cordelia has our power, Cordelia's queen.
    Speak, is not that the noble suffering Edgar?

GLOSTER: My pious son, more dear than my lost eyes.

LEAR: I wronged him too, but here's the fair amends.

EDGAR: Your leave, my liege, for an unwelcome message.
    Edmund (but that's a trifle) is expired.
    What more will touch you, your imperious daughters
    Goneril and haughty Regan, both are dead,
    Each by the other poisoned at a banquet.   130
    This, dying, they confessed.

CORDELIA: O fatal period of ill-governed life!

LEAR: Ingrateful as they were, my heart feels yet
    A pang of nature for their wretched fall.
    But, Edgar, I defer thy joys too long.
    Thou served'st distressed Cordelia. Take her crowned,
    The imperial grace fresh blooming on her brow.
    Nay, Gloster, thou hast here a father's right,
    Thy helping hand to heap blessings on their heads.

KENT: Old Kent throws in his hearty wishes too.   140

EDGAR: The gods and you too largely recompense
    What I have done. The gift strikes merit dumb.

CORDELIA: Nor do I blush to own myself overpaid
    For all my sufferings past.

GLOSTER: Now, gentle gods, give Gloster his discharge.

LEAR: No, Gloster, thou hast business yet for life.
    Thou, Kent and I, retired to some cool cell
    Will gently pass our short reserves of time
    In calm reflections on our fortunes past,
    Cheered with relation of the prosperous reign   150
    Of this celestial pair. Thus our remains
    Shall in an even course of thought be passed.
    Enjoy the present hour, nor fear the last.

142. Edgar is left speechless by Lear's generosity.

145. *discharge* – permission to die

Related Readings

EDGAR: Our drooping country now erects her head,
        Peace spreads her balmy wings, and Plenty blooms.
        Divine Cordelia, all the gods can witness
        How much thy love to empire I prefer!
        Thy bright example shall convince the world
        (Whatever storms of Fortune are decreed)
        That truth and virtue shall at last succeed.   160

                    Exeunt omnes.

                      FINIS.

                  ❧ ❧ ❧

Write a position paper in which you agree or disagree with the opinion expressed in the following quotation. Provide support for your position.

"The King and Cordelia ought by no means to have died, and therefore Mr. Tate has very justly altered that particular, which must disgust the Reader and Audience to have Virtue and Piety meet so unjust a Reward."

                    – Charles Gildon, British essayist (1710)

In groups, prepare a video or live presentation of Tate's ending of the play. You need not memorize the lines, but you should retain the essence of the speeches.

Why LEAR Must DIE

by Victor Hugo

Victor Hugo (1802–1885), French novelist and author of
Les Miserables, *was one of the first to object to Nahum Tate's
happy ending for* King Lear. *In this poem, Hugo explains why
Shakespeare's ending makes more sense.*

to live after the flight of the angel
to be the father orphaned of his child
to be the eye that no longer has light
to be the deadened heart that knows no more joy

from time to time
to stretch the hands into obscurity and try
to reclasp a being who was there
(where then can she be?)

to feel himself forgotten in that departure
to have lost all reason for being here below
to be henceforth a man who goes
to and fro before a sepulchre
not received, not admitted

this is indeed a gloomy destiny

thou hast done well, poet,
to kill this old man.

According to Hugo, why must Lear die? Do you agree with Hugo's opinion? Explain.

Write a poem in which you present your view on whether Lear must die.

Related Readings

by Anna Jameson

Cordelia

*In this selection, Irish writer Anna Jameson (1794–1860)
explores the enigmatic appeal of Cordelia.*

There is in the beauty of Cordelia's character an effect too sacred for words, and almost too deep for tears; within her heart is a fathomless well of purest affection, but its waters sleep in silence and obscurity—never failing in their depth and never overflowing in their fulness. Everything in her seems to lie beyond our view, and affects us in a manner which we feel rather than perceive. The character appears to have no surface, no salient points upon which the fancy can readily seize: there is little external development of intellect, less of passion, and still less of imagination. It is completely made out in the course of a few scenes, and we are surprised to find that in those few scenes there is matter for a life of reflection, and materials enough for twenty heroines. If *Lear* be the grandest of Shakespeare's tragedies, Cordelia in herself, as a human being governed by the purest and holiest impulses and motives, the most refined from all dross of selfishness and passion, approached near to perfection; and, in her adaptation as a dramatic personage to a determinate plan of action, may be pronounced altogether perfect. The character, to speak of it critically as a poetical conception, is not, however, to be comprehended at once, or easily; and in the same manner Cordelia, as a woman, is one whom we must have loved before we could have known her, and known her long before we could have known her truly....

Amid the awful, the overpowering interest of the story, amid the terrible convulsions of passion and suffering, and pictures of moral and physical wretchedness which harrow up the soul, the tender influence of Cordelia, like that of a celestial visitant, is felt and acknowledged without being quite understood. Like a soft star that shines for a moment from behind a stormy cloud, and the next is swallowed up in tempest and darkness, the impression it leaves is beautiful and deep, but vague....

> Everything in her seems to lie beyond our view, and affects us in a manner which we feel rather than perceive. The character appears to have no surface, no salient points upon which the fancy can readily seize....

It appears to me that the whole character rests upon the two sublimest principles of human action—the love of truth and the sense of duty; but these, when they stand alone, are apt to strike us as severe and cold. Shakespeare has, therefore, wreathed them round with the dearest attributes of our feminine nature, the power of feeling and inspiring affection. The first part of the play shows us how Cordelia is loved, the second part how she can love....

In Cordelia, it is not the external colouring or form, it is not what she says or does, but what she is in herself, what she feels, thinks, and suffers, which continually awaken our sympathy and interest. The heroism of Cordelia is ... passive and tender—it melts into our heart; and in the veiled loveliness and unostentatious delicacy of her character there is an effect ... profound and artless.... If Cordelia reminds us of anything on earth, it is of one of the Madonnas in the old Italian pictures ... ; and as that heavenly form is connected with our human sympathies only by expression of maternal tenderness or maternal sorrow, even so Cordelia would be almost too angelic, were she not linked to our earthly feelings, bound to our very hearts, by her filial love, her wrongs, her sufferings, and her tears. ■

Jameson suggests that Cordelia, as a person, "may be pronounced altogether perfect." To what extent do you agree or disagree with this view? Explain.

Imagine that each of the paragraphs in this selection were spoken in response to questions posed during a media interview. Write the questions that would have prompted Jameson to respond the way she did.

Calm After Storm

by Frank Yerby

*To keep himself from thinking about the storm within himself,
Lear braves the physical storm around him. In this poem,
American writer Frank Yerby (1916–1991) evokes a similar
internal turmoil and the calm that follows it.*

Deep in my soul there roared the crashing thunder,
And unseen rain slashed furrows in my face;
The lightning's flame with tendrils fine as lace,
Etched intricate designs, too keen for wonder
Upon my dull-eyed soul. And that rich plunder
Of stolen joys, snatched in the little space,
Between the dawn and dark, had caught the pace,
This rip-tide of the heart, and was drawn under.

But this slow calm, this torpid lack of caring,
Creeping along, a drugged dream of content,
Kills no less surely than the storm's duress;
Better the winds, like thin whip-lashes sparing
No proud young heart until their force is spent,
Than this vague peace, akin to nothingness.

In what way is the storm that rages within the speaker similar to a physical storm?

What similarities does the speaker in this poem share with Lear?

WHY KING LEAR IS THE CRUELLEST PLAY

by Frank Kermode

English scholar and critic Frank Kermode (b. 1919) argues that of all Shakespeare's tragedies, King Lear *is the cruellest and the one that has the most horrific images. Yet it continues to fascinate readers and audiences. How do we account for the appeal of this truly troubling play?*

*K*ing *Lear* is the most terrible of Shakespeare's tragedies, yet it begins like a folktale. An irritable old king decides to divide his kingdom between his three daughters, but he makes it a condition that they should take part in a competition, to show which of them loves him most. The two elder daughters—shallow, flashy types—perform without reluctance, but the youngest daughter simply won't play. So the furious old man disinherits his favourite daughter and leaves all his lands and his power to the other two, reserving to himself only the external trappings of kingship. He plans to divide his time between the houses, or castles, of the two wicked daughters. But soon he finds that they don't want him or his followers. He becomes homeless, wandering without shelter in bleak weather. He takes refuge in a hovel, where he meets a naked madman. Eventually, he's reunited with the daughter who really loves him, but by that time he's mad. He barely has time to recognise her, anyway, before she dies, and then he dies, too.

With this story Shakespeare interweaves another, again about a father and his children. A bastard son plots against his legitimate elder brother. The good son,

Edgar, is forced to flee. He adopts various disguises, including that of a naked madman, whom Lear encounters in the hovel. Meanwhile, the bastard son Edmund stops at nothing. He makes love to both the wicked daughters of the king but, worse than that, he makes no attempt to intervene when a horrible punishment is inflicted on his father, the Earl of Gloucester, for the Earl of Gloucester has his eyes torn out.

So the fairy story turns into a horror story, an account of cruelty and protracted suffering. Now, it would be monstrous to suggest that it's the story of a foolish old man being paid out for his follies. That's not what tragedy is about. Perhaps it's about making us look steadily, if only for a moment, at certain things that we prefer not to look at—death, for instance, or the way the world works, which is never the way we want it to work. Lear abandons his responsibilities and thinks that he can retain the name and all the additions of a king. He's wrong. He's not wicked. But then he begins a descent into privation—without shelter, without clothes, without the sanctions of a human society, even without ordinary human language. The play is full of strange gabble. There's the Court fool, traditionally

185

a mixture of craziness and shrewdness, sometimes impudent, sometimes obscene; there's Lear himself, raving sometimes, sometimes fantasticating; and there's Edgar as Poor Tom, imitating the patter of a naked Bedlam lunatic.

While Tom raves, the king descends into madness. He learns something on the way. He learns that human beings exist in utter desolation. But pity is not enough. He feels the need to identify himself with the naked, with Poor Tom, and he tears at his clothes. Later, when he's reunited with his daughter Cordelia, she takes great pains to dress him again according to his condition. But then she dies, his greatest loss, and we see him for the last time, fumbling with his clothes before he dies.

We're used to images of horror on the television and in the newspapers—war and famine, senility, concentration camps; we've domesticated them. We look at them and wait for the next programme. It may be the purpose of *King Lear* to defamiliarise those images of horror. Of course, it can't explain them—that's up to us—and if we want to, we can resist; we can turn them back into comfortable television images.

The history of this play could very well be written in terms of the way in which people have resisted it—resisted its assault on their comfortable notions of natural and social justice. It presents a world wildly at odds with the world that they would prefer to live in. And even in Shakespeare's own time, it seems that there may have been some resistance, that one or two of the scenes may have been thought too mad or too painful for performance. One such scene is in the hovel where Lear makes the Madman and the Fool act as judges in the trial of his two wicked daughters. The daughters have to be played by stools.

The great critic Samuel Johnson was one who resisted this play. In fact, he says he found it so painful that he could hardly bear even to read it. He thought that the death of Cordelia was contrary to the natural ideas of justice, and I think he was even more shocked that, in all the other versions of the Lear story, Cordelia survives. Only in Shakespeare's is she murdered.

Another famous and very bitter resister was Tolstoy. He repeatedly attacked *King Lear*. George Orwell suggested that one reason for this obsession could have been that Tolstoy was half conscious of his own resemblance to the king. Anyway, Tolstoy preferred the early, pre-Shakespearian version of the play, in which everything comes out all right and divine and human justice prevail. He thought Shakespeare's play was wicked and worthless and believed, too, that anybody who thought otherwise was the victim of a vast cultural conspiracy.

But whatever we think of these matters, we know that we can't count on divine or human justice to intervene in the worst moments of life, and what *King Lear* tries to do is to make us give our real assent to that knowledge. That's why it's the cruellest play. And its great climax and, to my mind, the supreme stretch of Shakespeare's

EVEN IN SHAKESPEARE'S OWN TIME, IT SEEMS THAT THERE MAY HAVE BEEN SOME RESISTANCE, THAT ONE OR TWO OF THE SCENES MAY HAVE BEEN THOUGHT TOO MAD OR TOO PAINFUL FOR PERFORMANCE.

imagination is the scene between the crazed king and the blind Gloucester at Dover.

Gloucester is patient under horrible teasing, but he wants to die. He tells Edgar that, rather than continue his stumbling flight, he'll sit down and rot, but Edgar won't have it. "Men must endure / Their going hence, even as their coming hither. / Ripeness is all. Come on," he says (5.2.10–12). And on they go. The old man must pass through all the prescribed stages. There's no short cut to nothingness.

Certain words echo through this play. "Nothing" is one of them; "eyes" is another. And clothes is another repeated idea. Nowadays splendid clothes aren't for every day, but in Shakespeare's time they were both more ostentatious and more common. They are symbols of wealth and power and sex—all the things that Poor Tom lacks as he faces the storm.

Lear develops quite a philosophy of clothes. Because he's obsessed with justice, he thinks most of the gowns of judges and of court officials. He addresses an imaginary beadle whipping a whore. "Strip thy own back," he says; "Thou hotly lusts to use her in that kind for which thou whipp'st her.... Through tatter'ed clothes small vices do appear. Robes and furr'ed gowns hide all." And under the furred gown is the naked body: "poor, bare, forked animal"(3.4.104).

Shakespeare's England still entertained the old doctrine of the king's two bodies. One body is identified with his dignity, his inherited and God-given authority, and that body is immortal. The king is dead; long live the king! But the other body is mortal. At his funeral, his mortal body lies naked in the coffin. His immortal body is represented by an effigy wearing his crown and robes.

Lear never sorted out his two bodies. As one of his cruel daughters said, "he hath ever but slenderly known himself"—and it's true. He thinks that he can retain the dignity with his mortal body. We see that mortal body stripped of its "additions," stripped of its dignity. When Lear was king, he thought he could command love, measure it and reward it accordingly. Now he's handed over that power to his two wicked daughters. It's they who now can ration out love. Which of them loves him better? Which will allow him 50 followers? But they reply: "Why do you need 50 followers? Why not 25?"

What are we to make of these villains? Edmund and the two sisters are wantonly cruel and self-seeking, and that's obvious. But what about their servant, Oswald? He's simply there to fetch and carry—a trivial part, and it could have stayed trivial, but he becomes a very important representative of another sort of evil. It's the kind of evil that Hannah Arendt, thinking of Adolf Eichmann and other people of his kind, had in mind when she spoke of "the banality of evil," the evil that is practised by those who simply carry out and augment the horrors that their masters have devised. It's of such people that Kent is thinking when he says: "Such smiling rogues as these, / Like rats, oft bite the holy cords atwain / Which are too intrince to unloose" (2.2.68–70).

Love and mutual respect are the holy cords, and there's always an Oswald ready to gnaw at them. He lives, like his masters,

> *THE OLD MAN MUST*
> *PASS THROUGH ALL THE*
> *PRESCRIBED STAGES.*
> *THERE'S NO SHORT CUT*
> *TO NOTHINGNESS.*

187

Henry Irving as King Lear by Sir Bernard Partridge (1861–1945)

in a state of nature where man is a wolf to man. That is the way the wicked always do live in Shakespeare. Of course, in the end they're destroyed, but so is Lear, so is Gloucester, and so is Cordelia—the sinned against as well as the sinning.

Such is the injustice we prefer not to look at. The remedy seems to be patience. Like Job, Lear is tried to the uttermost, but, unlike Job's, his losses aren't made good. And the play often reminds us that this is the way the world ends, not in restored happiness but in dismay. It speaks of the horror of the last days which, according to the Bible, must precede the end of time. Unnaturalness between the child and the parent, death, dearth, dissolutions of ancient amities—and at the end, as the old king deludes himself into thinking that Cordelia is still alive, Kent asks: "Is this the promised end?" and Edgar echoes him: "Or image of that horror?"(5.3.303–304)

An image, then, of the end—of the end of the world, of the end of ourselves, which for each individual amounts to the same thing. It's not surprising that Dr. Johnson found this play contrary to the natural ideas of justice. All through the play people are looking at the state of their world and trying to find evidence that it is just. When something that seems fair happens, a character says: "This shows you are above, You justicers," but to King Lear the justices are rogues, thieves in fur gowns. And if it weren't for the fidelity of Kent and the charity of Cordelia, we might think that the play was dismissing the whole notion of justice as fraudulent, as if under the fine words, as under the fine clothes, there was nothing but greed and lust.

So *King Lear* isn't just a play about a foolish king. It is about a king who loses his palace and his crown and his robes, and finds himself an unsheltered mortal. And it's also about a man without his dignity, lurking in hovels, without authority, without reason. We all live in societies that depend upon our belief in them and the belief of others. Without that belief they afford no shelter. I think Shakespeare, in his greatest years, was much preoccupied with that theme. He wanted here to express it unequivocally—if necessary, cruelly. Sanity, dignity and love—these depend upon a structure of belief which might even be a structure of illusion. He shows us the rats gnawing at the holy cords and the collapse of the structure, which is like the end of a world. In that situation we find ourselves naked, blind, deprived of reason. We babble at the dialects of privation. Our life is as cheap as a beast's. And that's why *King Lear* is the cruellest play. "Thou must be patient," says the mad Lear to the blind Gloucester. "We came crying hither. Thou know'st, the first time that we smell the air / We wawl and cry" (4.6.183–185). But Gloucester has no eyes and cannot cry.

And to the king himself the world has become an instrument of torture. "O, let him pass!" says Kent. "He hates him / That would upon the rack of this tough world / Stretch him out longer"(5.3.365–367). And the king says that he is bound upon a wheel of fire. So—we leave the theatre, switch off the television, and return to our temporary certainties and devices by which we make the world familiar and acceptable, but it seems right that for a moment we should have had a glimpse of it as it appeared to the stripped king. ■

Kermode maintains that the "history of the play could very well be written in terms of the way in which people have resisted it." Outline the various reasons why different people have objected to it. Is there any one opinion that you agree with most? Which do you agree with least? Explain.

Summarize briefly how Kermode arrives at the conclusion that *King Lear* is the cruellest play. What do you find most or least convincing about his arguments? Explain.

                                                                    Related Readings

REVIEWERS

The publishers and editors would like to thank the following educators for contributing their valuable expertise to the development of the *Global Shakespeare Series*:

Nancy B. Alford
Sir John A. Macdonald High
  School
Hubley, Nova Scotia

Philip V. Allingham, Ph.D.
Golden Secondary School
Golden, British Columbia

Francine Artichuk
Riverview Senior High
Riverview, New Brunswick

Carol Brown
Walter Murray Collegiate Institute
Saskatoon, Saskatchewan

Rod Brown
Wellington Secondary School
Nanaimo, British Columbia

Beverley Calabrese
Minto Memorial High School
Minto, New Brunswick

Joan Connell
Charlottetown Rural High School
Charlottetown, Prince Edward
  Island

Brian Dietrich
Queen Elizabeth Senior Secondary
Surrey, British Columbia

Alison Douglas
McNally High School
Edmonton, Alberta

Kimberley A. Driscoll
Adam Scott Collegiate
Peterborough, Ontario

Burton Eikleberry
Grants Pass High School
Grants Pass, Oregon

Gloria Evans
Lakewood Junior Secondary
  School
Prince George, British Columbia

Graham T. Foster
Calgary Catholic School District
Calgary, Alberta

Catherine Foy
Cobourg D.C.I. East
Cobourg, Ontario

Professor Averil Gardner
Memorial University
St. John's, Newfoundland

Joyce L. Halsey
Lee's Summit North High School
Lee's Summit, Missouri

Carol Innazzo
St. Bernard's College
West Essendon, Victoria, Australia

Winston Jackson
Belmont Secondary School
Victoria, British Columbia

Marion Jenkins
Glenlyon-Norfolk School
Victoria, British Columbia

Sharon Johnston, Ph.D.
Maynard Evans High School
Orlando, Florida

Jean Jonkers
William J. Dean Technical
  High School
Holyoke, Massachusetts

Beverly Joyce
Brockton High School
Brockton, Massachusetts

Judy Kayse
Huntsville High School
Huntsville, Texas

Doreen Kennedy
Vancouver Technical Secondary
  School
Burnaby, British Columbia

Betty King
District 3
Corner Brook, Newfoundland

Dan Kral
Regina Catholic School Education
  Centre
Regina, Saskatchewan

Kathryn Lemmon
James Fowler Senior High
Calgary, Alberta

Ed Metcalfe
Fleetwood Park Secondary School
Surrey, British Columbia

Janine Modestow
William J. Dean Technical High
  School
Holyoke, Massachusetts

Mary Mullen
Morell Regional High School
Morell, Prince Edward Island

Steve Naylor
Salmon Arm Senior Secondary
  School
Salmon Arm, British Columbia

Kathleen Oakes
Implay City Senior High School
Romeo, Michigan

Carla O'Brien
Lakewood Junior Secondary
  School
Prince George, British Columbia

Bruce L. Pagni
Waukegan High School
Waukegan, Illinois

Larry Peters
Lisgar Collegiate
Ottawa, Ontario

Margaret Poetschke
Lisgar Collegiate
Ottawa, Ontario

Jeff Purse
Walter Murray Collegiate Institute
Saskatoon, Saskatchewan

Grant Shaw
Elmwood High School
Winnipeg, Manitoba

Debarah Shoultz
Columbus North High School
Columbus, Indiana

Elaine Snaden
Windsor Board of Education
Windsor, Ontario

Tim Turner
Kiona-Benton High School
Benton City, Washington

James Walsh
Vernon Township High School
Vernon, New Jersey

Brian T.W. Way, Ph.D.
Oakridge Secondary School
London, Ontario

Edward R. Wholey
Sir John A. Macdonald High
  School
Halifax, Nova Scotia

Garry Williamson
Murdoch Mackay Collegiate
Winnipeg, Manitoba

Beverley Winny
Adam Scott Secondary School
Peterborough, Ontario

About the Series Editors

Dom Saliani, Senior Editor of the *Global Shakespeare Series*, is the Curriculum Leader of English at Sir Winston Churchill High School in Calgary, Alberta. He has been an English teacher for over 25 years and has published a number of poetry and literature anthologies.

Chris Ferguson is the Curriculum Director for the Central Texas Tech Prep Consortium in Temple, Texas. Formerly the Department Head of English at Burnet High School in Burnet, Texas, she has taught English, drama, and speech communications for over 15 years.

Dr. Tim Scott is an English teacher at Melbourne Grammar School in Victoria, Australia, where he directs a Shakespeare production every year. He wrote his Ph.D. thesis on Elizabethan drama.

ACKNOWLEDGMENTS

Permission to reprint copyrighted material is gratefully acknowledged. Every reasonable effort has been made to contact copyright holders. Any information that enables the publishers to rectify any error or omission will be welcomed. Selections may retain original spellings, punctuation, and usage.

On Sitting Down to Read King Lear Once Again by John Keats. Public domain. *Student Matinee, Stratford* by Margaret Stinson which appeared in SOULDUST AND PEARLS, OCTE 1981 Poetry Anthology. Copyright © 1981. Published by Belsten Publishing Ltd., Ontario. *Caporushes* in ENGLISH FAIRYTALES retold by Flora Annie Steel. First published by Macmillan & Co., 1918. *King Lear in Respite Care* from MORNING IN THE BURNED HOUSE by Margaret Atwood. Copyright © 1995. Used by permission, McClelland & Stewart, Inc. *The Canadian Publishers. Nothing Shall Come of Nothing* reprinted by permission of Louisiana State University Press from THE QUONDOM WIVES by Mairi MacInnes. Copyright © 1993 by Mairi MacInnes. *Wise Enough to Play the Fool* from ASIMOV'S GUIDE TO SHAKESPEARE VOLUME I by Isaac Asimov. Copyright © 1970 by Isaac Asimov. Used by permission of Doubleday, a division of Bantam Doubleday Dell Publishing Group, Inc. *Send in the Clowns* by Goenawan Mohamad. Published in TENGGARA, No. 27, 1990. Refrain by Mary Jo Salter. First published in THE KENYON REVIEW—New Series, Spring 1981, Vol. III, No. 2. *Goneril* by Karel Čapek from APOCRYPHAL STORIES by Karel Čapek. Copyright © Karel Čapek. Reprinted by permission. *I Dream of Lear* by Jerry W. Ward, Jr. First printed in OBSIDIAN II: BLACK LITERATURE IN REVIEW, Spring 1988, Vol. 3, No. 1. Reprinted by permission. *The Blind Leading the Blind* reprinted by permission of Louisiana State University Press from ALIVE TOGETHER: NEW AND SELECTED POEMS, by Lisel Mueller. Copyright © 1996 by Lisel Mueller. *A Dog, a Horse, a Rat* by A.S. Byatt reprinted by permission of The Peters Fraser and Dunlop Group Limited on behalf of: ©: as printed in TIMES LITERARY SUPPLEMENT, May 24, 1991, p. 22. *The Happy Ending* King Lear by Nahum Tate. Public domain. *Why Lear Must Die* by Victor Hugo. Public domain. *Cordelia* from SHAKESPEARE'S HEROINES by Anna Jameson, 1913. Public domain. *Calm After Storm* © 1963 by Frank Yerby. Reprinted by permission of William Morris Agency, Inc. on behalf of the author. *Why King Lear Is the Cruellest Play* by Frank Kermode reprinted by permission of The Peters Fraser and Dunlop Group Limited on behalf of: ©: as printed in THE LISTENER, Vol. 108, No. 2778, September 1982, pp. 13 and 14. *Lear* by Ruth E. Bell, in THE SHAKESPEARE NEWSLETTER, Vol. XXX:1, No. 162, p. 3., February 1980, Louis Marder, editor. Reprinted by permission.

ARTWORK

Yuan Lee: cover, 16, 42–43, 48, 60–61, 72, 82–83, 96, 112–13, 126, 140–41, 183; **Folger Shakespeare Library**, reprinted with permission: title page of *King Lear* from the Second Quarto (1619), 10; first page of *King Lear* from the First Folio (1623), 11; football players from Henry Peacham's *Minerua Britanna* (1612), 35; "May not an ass know ..." from *Mad Fashions, od fashions* (1642), 39; kite from Konrad Gesner's *Historia animalium* (1585–1604), 40; stocks from August Casimir Redel's *Apophtegmata symbolica*, 57; Fortune's wheel from *The hystorye, sege and dystruccyon of Troye* (1513), 58; bedlam beggar from Thomas Harman's *A caueat or warening* (1567), 59; bear-baiting from Charles Knight's *Pictorial Edition of the Words of Shakspere* (1839–43), 92; "She that herself will ..." from Henry Peacham's *Minerua Britanna* (1612), 101; **John James:** a performance at the Globe Theatre from Shakespeare's Theatre (Simon and Schuster, 1994), 12; **Mike Reagan:** 14; **Nicholas Vitacco:** 15; **IGNITION Design and Communications:** series logo; marginal art: 18, 36, 37, 77, 110, 113, 141, 176; **Annouchka Galouchko:** 147; **France Brassard:** 150; **Odile Ouellet:** 155; **Carmelo Blandino:** 158; **Stuart McLachlan:** 161, 164; **Bruce Roberts:** 168; **Blair Drawson:** 170; **Pierre-Paul Pariseau:** 174; **Susan Leopold:** 184; from the **RSC Collection** with the permission of the Governors of the Royal Shakespeare Theatre: *Henry Irving as King Lear*, by Sir Bernard Partridge (1861–945), 188.